MW00447133

The Major Field Test (MFT) for MBA
Study Guide

Complete with Sample Questions
and
Key Business Concepts

Second Edition

James E. Phelan, MBA

Copyright © 2014, 2019
James E. Phelan
Practical Application Publications
All rights reserved.

No portion of this publication may be reproduced in any manner
without written permission of the author or publisher.

ISBN-10: 0-9779773-8-2

ISBN-13: 978-0-9779773-8-3

Dedication

To Prof. Roger Kiesel for his untiring dedication and inspiration

Dedication

About the Author

James E. Phelan earned his MBA at Franklin University, Ross College of Business in Columbus, Ohio. He is currently on staff at the Veterans Health Administration, Columbus, Ohio and is an online college instructor.

Disclaimer

The author is not affiliated with, or receiving compensation from the *ETS®* Major Field Test for the MBA. The information in this study guide is intended as peer support and of the author's own education and opinion, and not taken from *ETS®* Major Field Test for the MBA. Sample questions are made up and not taken from existing sample tests, or an actual ETS® Major Field Test for the MBA. Any information about the *ETS®* Major Field Test for the MBA was received from their website. This guide is meant to be helpful, not authoritative of the *ETS®* Major Field Test for the MBA.

*Second Edition – all mathematical questions accompanied with detailed solutions.

Table of Contents

"Success in business requires training and discipline and hard work. But if you're not frightened by these things, the opportunities are just as great today as they ever were."

-David Rockefeller

Introduction

When I discovered that I had to take the MFT for the MBA, I was quite nervous. I wondered how I would be able to gather up all the materials I needed to prepare myself. I looked all over the place for a comprehensive study guide and discovered there was none! In order to help prepare myself I read some texts from prior classes, and went to the library and reviewed reference business books that discussed concepts and key ratios. It was rough going through all the endless materials! I also completed sample test questions, but only a few questions were available online.

As a result of all my efforts, I made a commitment that I would assist future fellow graduate students by compiling an appropriate study guide so they would benefit from it. My intention was to narrow down the external legwork for them knowing they have enough on their plate already. I really wished I had this guide when I was studying for the exam, but what I did learn I now want to share.

So, here you have it – the first and only comprehensive study guide available to help you prepare for the MFT for the MBA. I formatted it in such a way that it would clearly help you in your study, increasing your ability to do better on the exam.

Chapter 1 is a helpful roadmap for taking the MFT and testing taking in general. It includes tips to getting though some of the nuances you may encounter before and during the exam. Chapter 2 provides key concepts with definitions that you will need to review in order to be more prepared for the exam. As a bonus, some concepts are accompanied with additional references, examples, and go-to websites so you can explore them in more depth. Chapter 3 provides key business ratios. Those are the measures you will need in order to complete many of the finance and accounting questions that may come up on the exam. Chapter 4 is what I consider the meat and potatoes of the guide. Here you will find over 120 sample questions to help you practice for the exam.

Finally, happy studies and the best of luck to you as you prepare for the MTF and in your future career in business management!

Chapter 1

Preparing for your exam

The *ETS®* Major Field Test for the Masters of Business Administration (MBA)

Most MBA graduate programs require a terminal exit exam to gauge students' comprehensive competency in the field of business management. The *ETS®* Major Field Test for the MBA is the only comprehensive national assessment for program evaluation of its kind. Most of the questions require knowledge of specific information drawn from business management, marketing, finance and managerial accounting, or a combination of these. *ETS®* Major Field Test website (2014) does provide a small sample of 37 test questions and answers. Total scores for the *ETS®* Major Field Tests are reported on a scale of 220–300 (*ETS®* Major Field Test for the MBA website, 2014). You will be able to use scrap paper and a pencil, however calculators are not permitted. To insure integrity, exams are proctored at designated test facilities; open books or materials are not permitted.

Multiple-choice

The Major Field Test for the MBA consists of 124 multiple-choice questions (*ETS®* Major Field Test for the MBA website, 2014). Always check the testing website and your university's instructions first as formats may change after the publication of this guide. All questions, even case study questions will be formatted in multiple-choice format. No questions will be formatted simply as true/false. You will have a choice of 4 (usually: a, b, c , or d) possible answers, but the key is to choose the *best* answer. That will be the correct answer. In most multiple-choice exams the potential answers follow a particular pattern – the correct answer, an answer that could be deemed close to the correct answer (but is wrong), one/two answers near the topic (but also wrong) and one that is usually far removed from the correct answer.

If you approach a question you are not sure of the answer, the best approach is reasoning rather than guessing. Make sure you answer *all* the questions, even if you are not completely sure of whether or not you have the correct answer. If you are not sure about a question you can always skip it and go back to it after you answered the ones you are sure of. It's best to save those for last, as they will require more thought and if you stay with them too long, you will stress yourself out. It's not worth it. Expect to be able to do any business math calculations by hand.

Case study questions

Case example questions provides a platform which tests your knowledge and understanding of key management principles. You will be expected to answer questions that display depth and quality of analysis. You will be able to demonstrate a clear understandings of critical strategic management issues. Finally, you will be able to produce answers that demonstrate knowledge of several areas of business comprehensively. The key is to read each case carefully and use the provided information in a way that will contribute to the best possible answer. Think of the case study questions as hints that provide you the answers.

Study time

I suggest scheduling time to prepare for the MFT for the MBA. For example, set aside at least one hour (more may be necessary) a day for study time. Schedule this like anything else that would be important in your life such as a doctor's appointment and put it in your Outlook, your alarm clock, or in an application reminder. I suggest starting this at least 6 weeks prior to the exam. Even though it may be tempting, do not let any other activities impede on your study time. This dedication will pay off as you will find yourself prepared for the test and not stressed in the end trying to cram everything in all at once.

Time management

It's important to maximize your time. Study during times when you are most refreshed and alert. Study in a way that provides breaks. Studying long periods of time does not necessary mean you will retain everything. Short breaks help you to refresh and come back to the material with a more focused look. Breaks can include getting up to get a small snack or refreshment, a walk, or doing light stretches. It's probably not a good idea to use breaks to get into other more thought provoking activities such as bill paying, handling a dispute, or other stressful activities.

Physical environment

Make sure your study environment is conducive. A good study area is free of external distractions and noise. It is best to use an unoccupied room, or reserved space at your local library. Most libraries have enclosed, secure study rooms. Check with the library first as these rooms often have to be reserved. Ensure that the climate is ideal, not too hot, or cold. Make sure you have snacks and beverages available and that you put your phone and other electronic devices away while you study.

Reading and other study methods

This guide is meant to be helpful, however it is not complete. It will be important for you to review previous course materials and books on business concepts. Creating your own study cards can also be helpful. I suggest purchasing index cards to help with this. After reading the materials, write the concept or question on one side of the index card, then turn it over and place the answer on the other side. This will give you a tool to test yourself. Read the question and see if you know the answer or not. Once you check your answer you will have either confirmation that you were correct, or a chance to refresh your memory with the correct answer. This method helps create a win-win situation for you.

Make sure you have a good understanding of key business concepts (many provided in this guide, see Chapter 2) and accounting and financial ratios (see Chapter 3) and how they are applied to business practice. Knowing how to calculate the ratios are not enough, you must know how they apply to real world business management practices.

Sample testing

A good way to help you with the major exam is to complete as many sample questions as you can. Even though the questions are not the exact ones on the exam, they will give you an opportunity to test yourself and to see how much you know and at the same time, lead you to study potential materials that you may need to know for the exam. I suggest completing the *ETS®* Major Field Test in Master of Business Administration Sample Questions found on their website (*ETS®* Major Field Test for the MBA website, 2014).

To help broaden the depth of sample questions provided by *ETS®*, this guide provides over 120 sample questions. These together will give you over 150 sample questions to answer before you take the official test.

Exam week

Here are a few things to follow the week prior to your exam:

- Make sure you have plenty of sleep and rest.

- Make sure that you eat good nutritious meals including fruits and vegetables. However, do not make any drastic changes to your diet. Avoid eating out at restaurants or eating seafood as you don't want to risk getting food poisoning the week before your exam! Research shows that those who have good nutritious intake are better prepared for activities involving thinking.

- Do not stay up very late cramming, or worrying about the exam. The week prior to the exam you should feel confident because you should already have dedicated time each day to your study.

- Make sure you know exactly when and where to report for your exam and what items you can and cannot take. You may have to look at the testing site on Google maps, or if you are in the local area, perhaps drive there and check it out. Most importantly, make sure you know where you are going and where to park. You do not want to be late because you had this wrong.

Day of exam

Here are a few things to follow the day of your examination:

- Make sure you get plenty of sleep the night before and give yourself plenty of time to wake up.

- Eat well, but don't overdo it. Don't try anything new on the day of exam (e.g. new caffeinated drink, new breakfast item, fruit you don't normally eat, etc.). The last thing you want is stomach problems, or the jitters as you go to your examination.

- Bring what you need. Most exam facilities will allow bottled water and light snacks. They usually provide a locker/key for you. You will likely get a break, so be prepared.

- Be on time! Make sure you leave in plenty of time to get there, not just on time, but early! Leave early just in case you may run in a traffic situation, or other problems. This will create less stress.

- Relax! Keep calm and do not try to cram any last minute material. You should be prepared by the day of exam. There should be nothing more you can cram in that will make a huge difference, so just relax!

Answering

- Read all the questions thoroughly and clearly. Do not breeze through them. Make sure you understand each question fully before answering.

- Remember, no questions will be formatted simply as true/false. You will have a choice of 4 possible answers, but the key is to choose the best answer. That will be the correct answer. In most multiple-choice exams the potential answers follow a particular pattern – the correct answer, an answer that could be deemed close to the correct answer (but is wrong), one/two answers near the topic (but also wrong, and one that is usually far removed from the correct answer.

- Ensure the best choice is made. Use the process of elimination. Remember some answers may be correct or partial correct, but there is only one *best* answer.

- Expect to be able to do some business math calculations by hand. You will be able to use scrap paper and a pencil, however calculators are not permitted.

- Remember, if you approach a question you are not sure of the answer, the best approach is reasoning rather than guessing. Make sure you answer *all* the questions, even if you are not completely sure of whether or not you have the correct answer. If you are not sure about a question, you can always skip it and go back to it after you answered the ones you are sure of.

Common mistakes

- A common mistake occurs when students do not read the exam questions completely. Do not focus on one or two key words or concepts, rather focus on the question as a whole. Look for qualifying words or phases, such as "pick the *best*," "what is *most likely*," "what would you *not* do," or "what is *not the best* solution," etc..

- Some questions have two or more parts. Some students only answer one part missing others. Make sure you answer all parts of the question sequentially.

- Misuse of time allotaction is also a common mistake. Some students spend too much time on some questions, while neglecting others. Make sure you keep an eye on the time elapsing during your test. Again, if you are struggling with one question, don't waste a lot of time, just come back to it after you've answered the others.

- Use all the time allotted. Do not rush through the test. Give each question careful time. Often questions are answered wrong, not because the student didn't know the answer, rather they rushed and overlooked something.

- Some students finish their test with unanswered questions. Make sure you check and see that all questions are answered before you turn it in. Don't waste a lot of time re-checking your answers, but do make sure you didn't miss anything. It's okay to do a random audit, that is go to any question re-read it and see if you would answer it the same way again, but limit it. Don't make the mistake to second-guess every answer you gave.

- Exam proctors will generally offer a mid-break that does not count against your testing time limit. These are generally not mandatory, but don't make the mistake of skipping the break. A break will give you a chance to refresh and revitalize, which will benefit you. Take the break, take your time, and relax.

Chapter 2

Key Business Concepts in Business Management

Key Business Concepts in Business Management

A

Acid-test ratio: the ratio of current assets and current liabilities (also called quick ratio). The ratio equals the sum of a company's cash, short-term investments and accounts receivable divided by its current liabilities. This ratio shows how well a business is able to cover its short-term obligations (liquidity). A quick ratio of 1.00 means that the most liquid assets of a business are equal to its total debts and the business will just manage to repay all its debts by using its cash, marketable securities and accounts receivable. A quick ratio of more than one indicates that the most liquid assets of a business exceed its total debts. On the opposite side, a quick ratio of less than one indicates that a business would not be able to repay all its debts by using its most liquid assets.

Action-centered leadership (John Adair's Model): represents 3 key balanced activities – achieving the *task*, building and maintaining the *team*, and developing the *individual*. The key is *balance* because if not equally weighed the model is ineffective. Therefore, leaders who spend time managing each of these elements will likely be more successful than those who focus mostly on only one element.

Activity-based costing (ABC): accounting system that recognizes a business firm's relationship between costs, activities and products, and through this relationship assigns indirect costs to products less arbitrarily than traditional methods. For a good ABC example, consider : http://accountingexample.com/activity-based-costing-example/

Actual cash value: the amount of money, less depreciation, that it would cost to replace something damaged beyond repair with a comparable item.

Advanced planning and scheduling software (APS): a type of system that tracks costs based on the activities that are responsible for driving costs in the production of manufactured goods. An APS allocates raw materials and production capacity optimally to balance demand and plant capacity. With APS systems project teams can maximize their efficiency and lower their production costs. By keeping a close eye on APS data, teams know whether or not they need to order more supplies, they can track how much of their budget they have used on the project and they can, in turn, end up profitable.

Adverse selection: the theory that poor quality goods are more likely to sell than good ones because some sellers want to get rid of products, and the buyers are unable to judge whether the quality or price are too low. Sellers are at an advantage because they have information about the product's quality that buyers don't. An example of an adverse selection would be purchasing a piece of equipment that will be phased out and therefore the parts will no longer available.

Affiliative leadership: leadership style focusing on renewing a sense of kinship and building trust among various factions whose cooperation is desirable for promoting the goals of the organization. These leaders tend to adopt an empathetic approach. However, in an effort to appease people and help them realize their true potential, there is a danger of the goals of the organization getting side tracked and poor performances going unchecked.

Agile manufacturing: flexible manufacturing practices utilizing processes, tools and training to meet the demands of customers by turning speed and agility into a key competitive advantage. An agile company is in a much better position to take advantage of short windows of opportunity and fast changes in customer demand.

Alpha rating: the return a security or portfolio would be expected to earn if the market's rate of return were zero. An alpha of 0.5 means that the stock/trust would outperform the market-based return by 0.5% (see also **beta rating**).

Anti-trust laws: laws that prevent monopolies in the United States. The intent is to encourage a competitive and accountable marketplace. In 2013, a judge ruled that Apple violated the federal antitrust law by playing an integral role in eliminating retail competition in the sale of e-books.

Ask: the net asset value of a mutual fund plus any sales charges.

Asymmetric information: information that differs between parties; results in situation where consumers, suppliers, and producers do not have the same information for which to base decisions on.

Attention management: management method of ensuring that employees are focused on their work and on organizational goals since inattentiveness results in wasted time. Attention management subscribes to the theory that winning and sustaining attention is by tapping into people's emotions.

Attitude survey: a series of marketing questions that tap into people's feelings toward a firm or product. Used for research to assess the feelings of a target audience toward a product, brand, or organization

Autocrat leadership: leadership style of taking total authority and control over decision-making. By virtue of their position, autocratic leaders not only control the efforts of the team, but monitors them for completion – usually under close scrutiny. Autocrat leaders are often responsible for business failures as their staff tends to remain passive and afraid to point out problems to the autocrat.

Average up: to purchase additional shares of a security whose price is rising at intervals during the price rise period. This is done with the intent to raise the average price paid for the stock.

Averaging: buying or selling of stocks at different times and at different prices to establish an average price

B

Back office: refers to general management or administrative staff who do not have direct dealings with the company's customers (see also **front office** and **middle office**).

Balanced scorecard: a strategic management planning system aligning business activities to the vision and strategy of the organization, improve internal and external communications, and monitor organization performance against strategic goals. A recent global study by Bain & Co finds that the Balanced Scorecard is one of the top-ten most widely used management tools around the world. The API Knowledge Hub includes many examples, white papers, research reports and best practice case studies on how businesses have put the Balanced Scorecard concept into practice: http://www.ap-institute.com/Balanced%20Scorecard.html

Example of Balance Scorecard

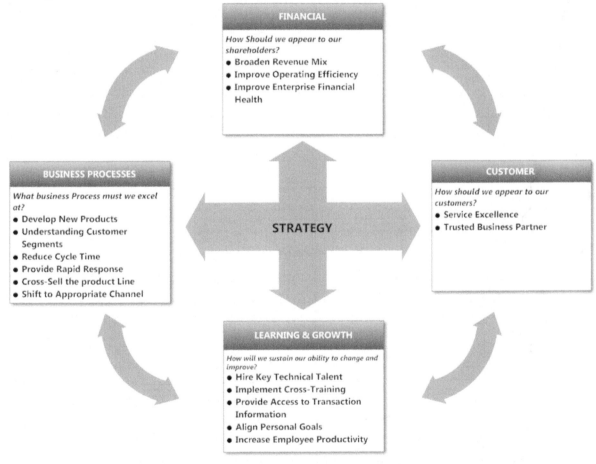

Adapted from the Balanced Scorecard by Robert S. Kaplan and Dave P. Norton. Harvard Business School Press. 1996.

http://www.smartdraw.com/software/balanced-scorecard-examples.htm

Balance Sheet: an income statement summarizing the financial affairs of a firm for a given period of time, such as a year. On the other hand, the balance sheet describes the financial conditions at one point in time, such as the last day of the year. The balance sheet shows the worth of the business at a particular time by listing its assets (things owned such as property, equipment) and money owned to the business, as well as liabilities (amounts owed by the business to others). The difference of these two amounts is the owner's equity (see example below).

Balance Sheet Example

Coca-Cola Company Consolidated Balance Sheet - January 31, 2001		
Current Assets	Dec. 31, 2001	Dec. 31, 1999
Cash & Equivalents	$1,819,000,000	$1,611,000,000
Short Term Investments	$73,000,000	$201,000,000
Receivables	$1,757,000,000	$1,798,000,000
Inventories	$1,066,000,000	$1,076,000,000
Pre-Paid Expenses	$1,905,000,000	$1,794,000,000
Total Current Assets	**$6,620,000,000**	**$6,480,000,000**
Long Term Assets	$8,129,000,000	$8,916,000,000
Property, Plant, & Equipment	$4,168,000,000	$4,267,000,000
Goodwill	$1,917,000,000	$1,960,000,000
Total Assets	**$20,834,000,000**	**21,623,000,000**
Current Liabilities		
Accounts Payable	$9,300,000,000	$4,483,000,000
Short Term Debt	$21,000,000	$5,373,000,000
Total Current Liabilities	**$9,321,000,000**	**$9,856,000,000**
Long-Term Liabilities		
Long-Term Debt	$835,000,000	$854,000,000
Other Liabilities	$1,004,000,000	$902,000,000
Deferred Long Term Liability Charges	$358,000,000	$498,000,000
Total Liabilities	**$11,518,000,000**	**$12,110,000,000**
Shareholders' Equity		
Common Stock	$870,000,000	$867,000,000
Retained Earnings	$21,265,000,000	$20,773,000,000
Treasury Stock	($13,293,000,000)	($13,160,000,000)
Capital Surplus	$3,196,000,000	$2,584,000,000
Other Stockholder Equity	($2,722,000,000)	($1,551,000,000)
Total Stockholder Equity	**$9,316,000,000**	**$9,513,000,000**

Below-the-line: used to describe a country's capital transactions, as opposed to its above-the-line, or revenue transactions.

Benchmark: a point of reference, or standard against which to measure business performance. Originally used for a set of computer programs to measure the performance of a computer against similar models, benchmark is now used more generally to describe a measure identified in the context of a benchmarking program.

Beta or beta coefficient: represents an estimate of the fluctuations in value of a stock in relation to the market as a whole. A high beta indicates that a stock is likely to be more sensitive to market movements and therefore has a higher risk. A beta below 1 can indicate either an investment with lower volatility than the market, or a volatile investment whose price movements are not highly correlated with the market.

Beta rating: utilities have a beta of less than 1. Conversely, most high-tech NASDAQ-based stocks have a beta greater than 1 since they offer a higher rate of return, yet are also risky. The market profile of all investable assets has a beta of 1.

Board of directors: governing body of incorporated firm. Members of the board are elected normally by stockholders of the firm to govern the firm and to look after their interests.

Board of trustees: governing body of a non-profit organization such as a charity, trust, or university. Members of the board are appointed rather than elected. Their roles are essentially to set the policies of the organization, and appoint (or fire) senior management personnel. The board is liable for the financial and other consequences of the organization's activities.

Bond: a person who invests in a bond is lending money to a company or government for a specified time with understanding it will be paid back with a fixed interest.

Bond Discount: the difference between the face value of a bond and the lower price at which it was issued.

Bond rating: the rating of the reliability of a company, government, or local authority that has issued a bond. The highest rating is AAA.

Bottleneck: an activity within an organization that has a lower capacity than preceding or subsequent activities, thereby limiting throughput. Bottlenecks are often the cause of a buildup of work in progress and of idle time.

Bottom-up approach: leadership approach that is consultative promoting employee participation at all levels in the decision-making and problem solving process. A bottom-up approach to leadership is associated with flat organizations and the empowerment of employees. It is accredited as encouraging creativity and flexibility.

Brand loyalty: brand loyalty is a result of consumer behavior affected by preferences. Loyal customers will consistently purchase products from their preferred brands, regardless of convenience or price. Companies will often use different marketing strategies to cultivate customers' loyalty through rewards programs or trials and incentives (e.g. free samples and gifts).

Brand positioning: the strategic development of a brand's position in the market by heightening customer perception of the brand's superiority over other brands of a similar nature. For example, Wendy's restaurants are now trying to build position over others by mass marketing their products as "...better"! In the past, Wendy's capitalized on positioning their burger brand by asserting it had more beef, therefore superior (see also **competitive strategy**).

Break-even: the point at which revenue from a product cancels out its costs.

Break-even chart: a management aid used in conjunction with break-even analysis to calculate the point at which fixed and variable production costs are met by incoming revenue. Lines are plotted to indicate expected sales revenue and production costs. The point at which the lines intersect marks the break-even point. A break-even chart like the one shown below, shows the Break-Even Point (BEP) as the intersection between the Total Revenue and Total Cost when plotted with the number of units on the x-axis. The Profit (or Loss) is also shown on the chart as Total Revenue - Total Cost.

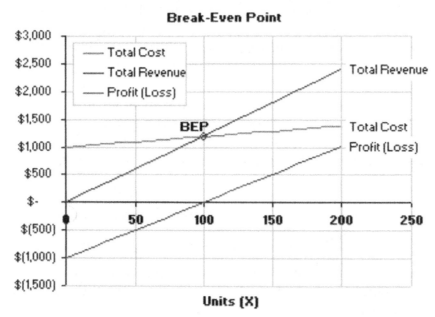

From: **http://www.vertex42.com/ExcelTemplates/breakeven-analysis.html**

Break-even point: the cost of an item plus the operating expenses associated with the item. Above this amount a profit is made, below it, a loss is incurred.

C

Capital flow: the movement of investments from one country to another.

Capitalization: a firm's value measured in its worth of stock and bonds issued.

Cash in: selling stock or other property for cash.

Cash management: strategy used by businesses to manage their cash flow in order to have more cash available for short-term investment. Strategy can include such things as accelerating cash receipts, prioritizing cash disbursements, and maintaining a cash balance to cover emergencies.

Category killer: is a major company (e.g. big box retail chain) that is more efficient, but less specialized than others, usually smaller merchants in the niche or industry. Category killers are a threat to smaller merchants because people tend to flock to the larger stores more often, based on their low cost strategies and wider distribution of stores.

Change management: a systematic approach to dealing with change, both from the perspective of an organization and on the individual level. A business practice of change management would be one that helps individuals and the organization transition from their current state to their desired state.

Channel management: a marketing process of identifying, reaching, and satisfying customers. One example would be where a firm attempts to reach a segment of customers by learning how that segment uses products and based on this information, utilize marketing strategies that would produce the most satisfaction to these customers.

Cognitive dissonance: marketing in a way to get customers to buy a product despite the fact that it may not necessarily be good for them (e.g. foods high in fat or sugar content) and the ability to help them work through this condition.

Competitive advantage: the advantage a firm has over its competitors, allowing it to generate greater sales or margins and/or retain more customers than its competition. Advantages include such things as the firm's cost structure, product offerings, distribution network and customer support (see also **value chain**).

Competitive intelligence: data gathered from rival companies in order to work on improving the organization's competitive capacity. This information can be critical in building strategies against rivals.

Competitive strategies: these are attributes companies embrace in their attempt to out perform rivals. Generic strategies are classified as: *differentiation*, *cost*, and *focus*:

Differentiation:

Broad differentiation strategy: one in which a business seeks to differentiate its products or services from their competitors in ways that attract the broadest spectrum of customers in an established industry. For example: BMW and Apple.

Cost:

Low-cost strategy: entails the process of appealing to the broad spectrum of potential buyers by being able to offer an overall low cost product or service. For example: Target and Wal-Mart.

Best-cost (provider) strategy: offers customers more value for their dollar, with a lot of emphasis on the low cost of the product or service in comparison to its high quality. For example: Ford with its Lincoln luxury models.

Focus:

A focused strategy on lower costs: is a brand positioning strategy that concentrates on out competing rivals by offering customized products or services at a lower cost to a smaller portion of the established buyers. For example: small retailers offering their own label or discounted line of products.

A focused strategy based on differentiation: one in which the focus is on a narrow segment of buyers who are offered a product or service that has been customized to meet their exact tastes and demands and supersedes what competitors are offering. For example, a successful niche retailer such as Talbots. Differentiation entails competing on the basis of value added to customers so that customers will pay a premium to cover higher costs.

Complementary goods: these are goods sold separately, but dependent on each other for sales. Examples of complementary goods include televisions and entertainment centers, or clothes and shoes.

Conflict management: management that aims to limit and control conflict in ways that will enhance effectiveness of the organization. There are 3 main philosophies of conflict management: (1) all conflict is bad and potentially destructive; (2) conflict is inevitable and managers should attempt to harness it positively; (3) conflict is essential to the survival of an organization and should be encouraged. Rahim theorized there are several approaches, yet there is no one best way to manage conflict. Some mangers like an *integration approach* as it involves openness, exchanging information, looking for alternatives, and examining differences to solve the problem in a manner that is acceptable to both sides in conflict.

Contingency theory: the theory that there is no single best way to organize or manage a company and that each company should be organized and structured to suit the technology used and the environment around it. The best way of organizing the company is contingent upon the internal and external situation of the company.

Corporation: a form of business organization offering limited liability to shareholders – no more money may be lost than has been invested.

Coupon rate: this is basically the interest rate paid to the holder and is also called the *nominal yield* or *yield rate*; this is stated on the bond and paid as described on the bond. For example, a bond that pays 5% has a coupon rate of 5%.

CPFR (Collaboration Planning, Forecasting and Replenishment): a business practice that combines the intelligence of multiple trading partners in the planning and fulfillment of the customer demand. CPFR links sales and marketing best practices to supply chain planning and execution processes. The objective is to increase availability to the customer while reducing inventory, transportation and logistics costs

Current assets: cash or items that can be converted into cash within a short period of time (e.g. one year). Types include:

> *Actual cash*: cash in checking and savings accounts

> *Marketable securities*: stocks, bonds, and other securities that can be quickly converted to cash

> *Accounts receivable*: funds owned by customers of the firm

> *Notes receivable*: value of all notes owed to the firm

> *Inventory*: cost of merchandise that the firm has for sale

Customer order cycle: the time customers are willing to wait.

D

Decision theory: encompasses both formal mathematical and statistical approaches to solving decision problems, using quantitative techniques such as probability and game theory. Decision theory divides decisions into three classes (1) *Decisions under certainty*: where a manager has far too much information to choose the best alternative. (2) *Decisions under conflict*: where a manager has to anticipate moves and counter-moves of one or more competitors. (3) *Decisions under uncertainty*: where a manager has to dig up a lot of data to make sense of what is going on and what it is leading to.

Decentralization: brings delegation of decision-making to subunits of an organization rather that it being solely at the top. Generally this works best when subunits are autonomous and their costs and profits are independently measured.

Decision tree: a schematic tree-shaped diagram used to determine a course of action or show a statistical probability. Each branch of the decision tree represents a possible decision or occurrence. The tree structure shows how one choice leads to the next, and the use of branches indicates that each option is mutually exclusive.

Example of a Decision Tree

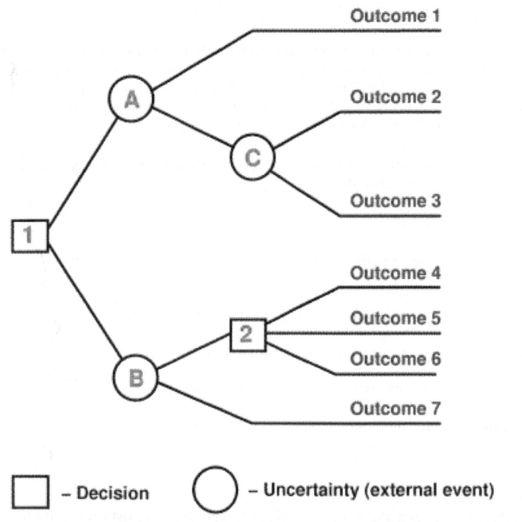

From: http://www.time-management-guide.com/decision-tree.html

Deconstruction: involves the breaking up of traditional business structures to meet the requirements of the modern economy. Deconstruction is necessary when systems are archaic and no longer effective.

Delphi technique: a widely used systematic forecasting method that involves structured interaction among a group of experts on a subject. The technique typically includes rounds of experts answering questions and giving justification for their answers, providing the opportunity between rounds for changes and revisions. The multiple rounds, which are stopped after a pre-defined criterion is reached, enable the group of experts to arrive at a consensus forecast on the subject being discussed.

Delta: the ratio comparing the change in the price of the underlying asset to the corresponding change in the price of a derivative. In terms of examples, a delta of 0.7 means that for every $1 the underlying stock increases, the call option will increase by $0.70. An option that changes in premium by $1 for every $2 in the price of the underlying security has a delta of 0.05.

Democratic leadership: leadership style where all individuals are involved in the decision-making process to determine what needs to be done and how it should be done, an advantage as this often creates job satisfaction because it fosters a sense of participation. On the other hand, decisions making and implementation are delayed compared to autocratic leadership because under this style more than one person is involved in decision making process.

Differential pricing: allows a company to adjust pricing based on various situations or circumstances. The price variations come in different forms, from discounts for a particular group of people to coupons or rebates for a purchase.

Diffusion of innovation theory: for any new product to be successful, it must attract *innovators* and *early adopters*, so that its acceptance or 'diffusion' moves on to *early majority*, *late majority*, and then on to *laggards*.

Discount: an amount subtracted from the price of a product or service which helps the buyer purchase at a lower cost and increases profits. The amount of interest charged on a note; also called a bank discount.

Dividend: money designed by the board of directors to be distributed among stockholders usually stated a dollar amount per share.

Dividend payout: the generated cash that a corporation issued to a shareholder as a dividend on the total number of shares. Depending on the structure of the stock issue, the dividend payout may involve all the net profit generated during the fiscal year, or be a portion of the net profit.

DuPont formula: method for assessing a company's return on equity (ROE) breaking it into three parts: Operating efficiency, which is measured by net profit margin; asset use efficiency, which is measured by total asset turnover; and financial leverage, which is measured by the equity multiplier. If ROE is unsatisfactory, the DuPont formula helps locate the part of the business that is underperforming.

E

Early adopter: a the minority group (about 14%) of population which, after innovators, is first to try new ideas, processes, goods and services. Early adopters generally rely on their intuition and vision, choose carefully, and have above-average education level.

Earnings per share (EPS): total earnings (minus dividends on preferred stock) divided by the number of shares outstanding. EPS is a good indicator of the company's performance and helpful when considering whether or not to invest in that company.

Economy of scale: economic principle stating that as the volume of production increases, the cost of producing each unit decreases. Economies of scale are the advantages of doing something on a large rather than a small scale. Economies of scale lower the unit cost of production. For example, producing 1,000 high quality copies of document on a modern dedicated in-house copier, is much cheaper (per copy) than ordering 100 copies of the document from a local printer.

Engagement: human resource management approach designed to ensure that employees are sincerely committed to their organization's goals and values, motivated to contribute the organization's success, and are able at the same time to enhance their own sense of well-being.

Equality: a principle of management where there is equal opportunity within the organization and avoidant of discrimination by age, race, sex, sexual orientation, disability, or religion.

Equilibrium price: the price at which the supply of goods matches demand.

Ex-coupon: a bond or preferred stock that does not include the interest payment or dividend when purchased or sold.

Exporting: the act of producing goods or services in one country and then selling or trading them abroad.

F

Factors of production: inputs that are used in the production of goods or services in the attempt to make profit. Factors of production include land, labor, capital and entrepreneurship.

Fair trade: an international business system by which countries agree not to charge import duties on some items imported from their trading partners.

Field trial: a process to test the physical or engineering properties of a product in order to identify and hash out any technical problems before marketing. Customers may be involved in some trials, for example, in testing things like new personal care products or certain foods. Field trials should not be confused with test marketing, which is used to determine the likely market for, and likely consumer response to, a new product or service.

First in, first out (FIFO): the cost of goods purchased first (first-in) is the cost of goods sold first (first-out). During periods of high inflation-rates, the FIFO method yields higher value of the ending inventory, lower cost of goods sold, and a higher gross profit (hence the higher taxable income) than that is yielded by the last-in first-out (LIFO) method (see also **last-in first-out (LIFO)**). A good, to easy-to-read article about FIFO can be found at: http://www.accountingexplanation.com/fifo_method.htm

First mover advantage: the advantage gained by the initial ("first-moving") significant occupant of a market segment. It follows the notion that being the first company to sell a new product may provide long-lasting benefits or competitive advantages.

Fishbone chart: also known as the cause-and-effect diagram, invented by Kaoru Ishikawa, this chart is used to identify all possible causes of a problem. The beginning of the chart is the "head" of the fish. A horizontal line extends from the head with diagonal lines on each side of it to denote the "fish bones." Using (creating) a fishbone diagram to analyze the probable steps leading to a problem can be a helpful tool in finding a solution. MindTools has a good tutorial on producing a Fishbone chart: http://www.mindtools.com/pages/article/newTMC_03.htm

Example

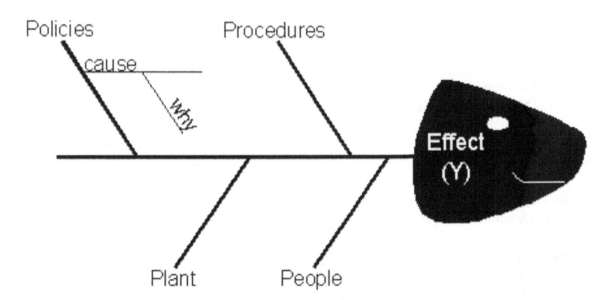

Once you have the branches labeled, begin brainstorming possible causes and attach them to the appropriate

branches. For each cause identified, continue to ask "why does that happen?" and attach that information as another bone of the category branch. This will help get you to the true drivers of a problem.

Ref: http://www.isixsigma.com/tools-templates/cause-effect/cause-and-effect-aka-fishbone-diagram/

Five forces that shape strategy (The Porter Model): Michael Porter's Harvard business model stating that the forces that shape strategy are: rivalry among competitors; bargaining power of buyers; threats of substitute products/services; bargaining power of suppliers; and threat of new entrants.

Fixed cost: a cost that does not vary depending on production or sales levels, such as rent, property tax, insurance, or interest expense.

Flow line production: a production method in which successive operations are carried out on a product in such a way that it moves through the factory in a single direction. Flow line production is most widely used in mass production on production lines. More recently, it has been linked with batch production. Inventory is often kept to the minimum necessary to ensure continued activity. Stoppages and interruptions to the flow indicate a fault, and corrective action can be taken.

Flow theory: a theory of the way in which people become engaged with, or disengaged from, change. The theory suggests that people harmonize in change situations, and open, honest, trusting relationships emerge. The theory recognizes the unpredictability and rigidity of human nature when faced with change.

Focus group: a marketing process where selected representative consumers or employees are used for the purposes of providing feedback on preferences and responses to a selected range of issues. A focus group generally operates with a facilitator who helps guide the discussion.

Forecasting: Estimating future trends by examining and analyzing available information. There are numerous techniques that can be used to accomplish the goal of forecasting. For example, a retailing firm that has been in business for 30 years can forecast its volume of sales in the coming year based on looking at historical data (see also **Quantitative research**).

Formal group: purposely designed group to accomplish an organizational objective or task. It is created via formal authority for some defined purpose.

Frequency analysis: a technique for comparing the number of opportunities to reach the same target audience in different media.

Fringe benefits: rewards given or offered to employees in addition to their wages or salaries and included in their employment contract. Fringe benefits range from share options, company cars, expense accounts, cheap loans, medical insurance, and other types of incentive plan to discounts on company products, subsidized meals, and membership of social and health clubs. Many of these benefits are liable for tax. In the United States, a cafeteria plan permits employees to select from a variety of such benefits, although usually some are deemed to be core and not exchangeable for others. Minor benefits, sometimes appropriated rather than given, are known as perks.

Front office: the staff members in the business who deal directly with customers and clients.

G

Game theory: used to represent conflicts and problems involved in formulating marketing and organizational strategy, with the goal of identifying and implementing optimal strategies. Game theory involves assessing likely strategies to be adopted by players in a given situation under a particular set of rules.

Gamma: A measurement of how fast delta changes, given a unit change in the underlying futures price. In a delta-hedge strategy, gamma is sought to be reduced in order to maintain a hedge over a wider price range. A consequence of reducing gamma, however, is that alpha too will be reduced.

GAP analysis: the comparison of actual performance with potential performance in this way: (1) listing of characteristic factors (such as attributes, competencies, performance levels) of the present situation ("what is"), (2) listing factors needed to achieve future objectives ("what should be"), and then (3) highlighting the gaps that exist and need to be filled. Gap analysis forces a company to reflect on who it is and ask who they want to be in the future.

Generic strategies: (see "**Competitive strategies**")

Global marketing: the process of conceptualizing and conveying a final product or service worldwide with strategies of reaching the international marketing community.

Globalization: denotes worldwide movement toward economic, financial, trade, and communications integration. Most markets use a hybrid approach to business practices, and are not totally homogenized.

Gross margin: in *Finance*, the gross margin is the difference between the interest rate paid by a borrower and the cost of the funds to the lender; in *Accounting*, the difference between revenue and cost of revenue expressed as a percentage; and in *Operations & Production*, the difference between the manufacturing cost of a unit of output and the price at which it is sold.

Gross profit method: a method used to estimate inventory value at cost which utilizes cost amounts.

Gross yield: the income return derived from securities before the deduction of tax.

Group-think: the tendency of members of a group to yield to the desire for consensus or unanimity at the cost of considering alternative courses of action. Group-think is said to be the reason why intelligent and knowledgeable people make disastrous decisions.

H

Harmonization: adjustment of differences and inconsistencies among different measurements, methods, procedures, schedules, specifications, or systems to make them uniform or mutually compatible.

Harvesting strategy: planned discontinuation of a product at the end of its life cycle, while extracting maximum profit from its sales. In this strategy, all marketing expenditure is gradually eliminated and the product is allowed to sell on its goodwill until sales revenue falls below a cutoff point (see also **Product life cycle)**.

Hedge: making an investment to reduce the risk of adverse price movements in an asset. Normally, a hedge consists of taking an offsetting position in a related security, such as a futures contract.

Horizontal integration: the acquisition of additional business activities that are at the same level of the value chain in similar or different industries. This can be achieved by internal or external expansion. Because the different firms are involved in the same stage of production, horizontal integration allows them to share resources at that level. If the products offered by the companies are the same or similar, it is a merger of competitors. If all of the producers of a particular good or service in a given market were to merge, it would result in the creation of a monopoly. Also called lateral integration.

Human capital: the employees of an organization. The term builds on the concept of capital as an asset of an organization, implying recognition of the importance and monetary worth of the skills and experience of its employees; measured through **human capital accounting** (see also). The set of skills which an employee acquires on the job, through training and experience, and which increase that employee's value in the marketplace is also considered part of human capital.

Human capital accounting: placing a financial figure on the knowledge and skills of an organization's employees or human capital.

Human resource accounting: the identification, recording, and reporting of the investment in, and return from the employment of the personnel within an organization

Human resource forecasting: for the sake of HR planning this is the prediction of future levels of demand for, and supply of, workers and skills at organizational, regional, or national level. A variety of techniques are used in manpower forecasting, including the statistical analysis of current trends and the use of mathematical models. At the national level, these include the analysis of census statistics; at the organizational level, projections of future requirements may be made from sales and production figures (see also **Human resource planning)**.

Human resource management: the function within an organization that focuses on recruitment of, management of, and providing direction for the people who work in the organization.

Human resource planning: the ongoing process of systematic planning to achieve optimum use of an organization's most valuable asset - its human resources. The objective of human resource planning is to ensure the best fit between employees and jobs, while avoiding manpower shortages or surpluses. The three key elements of the HR planning process are forecasting labor demand, analyzing present labor supply, and balancing projected labor demand and supply.

I

Import penetration: the degree to which one country's imports dominate the market share of those from other industrialized countries.

Import quota: the degree to which one country's imports dominate the market share of those from other industrialized countries.

Importing: the business of bringing goods or services into one country from another, in other words, international trade. The higher the value of imports entering a country, compared to the value of exports, the more negative that country's balance of trade becomes.

Income bond: a bond that a company repays only from its profits

Income fund: a fund that attempts to provide high income rather than capital growth.

Incorporated: formed into a legal corporation, incorporated entities have a legal status distinct from that of their owners, and limited liability.

Infinite capacity planning: a way of measuring potential future capacity whereby the actual capacity constraints of each individual workstation are not taken into account.

Information management: is a discipline that governs accountability structure and design, storage, movement, security, quality, delivery and usage of information required for management and business intelligence purposes.

Innovators: first buyers of new technologies (see also **Diffusion of innovation theory)**.

Inputs: resources such as people, raw materials, energy, information, or finance that are put into a system (such as an economy, manufacturing plant, computer system) to obtain a desired output. Inputs are classified under costs in accounting.

Insourcing: delegating a job to someone within a company, as opposed to someone outside of the company (outsourcing). One reason for insourcing to occur is if a company had previously outsourced a certain task, but was no longer satisfied with the work being done on that task, so the company could therefore insource the task and assign it to someone within the company who they feel will do a better job.

Intellectual property: intangibles owned by the business such as ideas that are patent, trade secrets, instructions, copyrights and trademarks, or ideas.

Interactive planning: approach that calls for actively involving all parties that are affected by the project at hand in the process of developing the steps and procedures that ultimately bring the plan to fruition.

Internal growth: organic growth created within a business, for example, by inventing new products and so increasing its market share, producing products that are more reliable, offering a more efficient service than its competitors, or being more aggressive in its marketing.

Internal marketing: involves the creation of an internal market by dividing departments into business units, with control over their own operations and expenditure, with attendant impacts on corporate culture, politics, and power. Internal marketing also involves treating employees as internal customers with the goal of increasing employees' motivation and focus on customers.

Issued shares: the number of authorized shares that are sold to and held by the shareholders of a company, regardless of whether they are insiders, institutional investors or the general public. Also referred to as "issued stock."

J

Joint bond: a bond that is guaranteed by a party other than the company or government that issued it.

Joint management: the overseeing and control of the affairs of an organization shared by two or more people.

K

Key account management: the management of the customer relationships that are most important to a company. Key accounts are those held by customers who produce the most profit for a company or have the potential to do so, or those who are of strategic importance. Development of these customer relations and customer retention is important to business success. Particular emphasis is placed on analyzing which accounts are key to a company at any one time, determining the needs of these particular customers, and implementing procedures to ensure that they receive premium customer service and to increase customer satisfaction.

Knowledge management: the coordination and exploitation of an organization's knowledge resources, in order to create benefit and competitive advantage.

L

Laggards: the last buyers of technology are referred to in marketing as laggards (see also **Diffusion of innovation theory**).

Laissez-faire leadership: a non-authoritarian leadership style. Laissez faire leaders try to give the least possible guidance to subordinates, and try to achieve control through less obvious means. They believe that people excel when they are left alone to respond to their responsibilities and obligations in their own ways.

Lambda: a ratio between the expected change in the price of an option and a one percent change in the expected volatility of the underlying asset.

Last in, last out: an asset-management and valuation method that assumes that assets produced or acquired last are the ones that are used, sold or disposed of first. (see also **First in, first out (FIFO)**)

Lead time: the amount of time that elapses between when a process starts and when it is completed. Businesses are motivated to reduce lead times in order to increase customer satisfaction.

Lean enterprise: an organizational model that strategically applies the key ideas behind lean production. A lean enterprise is viewed as a group of separate individuals, functions, or organizations that operate as one entity. The goal is to apply lean techniques that create individual breakthroughs in companies and to link these up and down the supply chain to form a continuous value stream to raise the whole chain to a higher level.

Lean production: a methodology aimed at reducing waste in the form of overproduction, excessive lead time, or product defects in order to make a business more effective and more competitive.

Lewin's stages of change: a three-stage theory of change commonly referred to as "Unfreeze," "Change," then "Freeze (or Refreeze)." "Unfreezing" stage involves moving ourselves, or a department, or an entire business towards motivation for change. The "change stage" occurs as we make the changes that are needed, and finally the "Freeze (or

Refreeze)" occurs when changes are accepted and become the new norm. Here, people form new relationships and become comfortable with their routines.

LLC: a **limited liability company** (**LLC**) is a flexible form of enterprise that blends elements of partnership and corporate structures. An LLC is not a corporation; it is a legal form of company that provides limited liability to its owners in the vast majority of United States jurisdictions. LLCs do not need to be organized for profit. In certain US states, businesses that provide professional services requiring a state professional license, such as legal or medical services, may not be allowed to form an LLC but required to form a very similar entity called a Professional Limited Liability Company (PLLC).

Limited partnership: is a form of partnership similar to a general partnership, except that in addition to one or more *general partners* (GPs), there are one or more *limited partners* (LPs). It is a partnership in which only one partner is required to be a general partner. The GPs are, in all major respects, in the same legal position as partners in a conventional firm (i.e. they have management control, share the right to use partnership property, share the profits of the firm in predefined proportions, and have joint and several liability for the debts of the partnership). As in a general partnership, the GPs have actual authority, as agents of the firm, to bind all the other partners in contracts with third parties that are in the ordinary course of the partnership's business.

Liquid assets: cash, or items that can be converted to cash quickly.

Liquidity: a firm is liquid if it has the ability to pay its bills as they come due.

M

Manufacturing cost: cumulative total of resources that are directly used in the process of making various goods and products.

Marginal pricing: the process of setting an item's price at the same level as the extra expense involved in producing another item. By using marginal cost pricing, a business helps keep their sales price down in order to encourage sales during slow periods or to gain market share.

Marginal revenue: the increase in revenue that results from the sale of one additional unit of output. Marginal revenue is calculated by dividing the change in total revenue by the change in output quantity. While marginal revenue can remain constant over a certain level of output, it follows the law of diminishing returns and will eventually slow down, as the output level increases. Perfectly competitive firms continue producing output until marginal revenue equals marginal cost.

Marketing mix: the marketing mix or four Ps— product, price, place (channels of distribution), and promotion— are adjusted so that the customer will buy the product and use it with a high level of satisfaction.

Marketing penetration pricing: the policy of pricing a product or service very competitively, and sometimes at a loss to the producer, in order to increase its market share.

Market segmentation: a marketing strategy that involves dividing a broad target market into subsets of consumers who have common needs and applications for the relevant goods and services. Depending on the specific characteristics of the product, these subsets may be divided by criteria such as age and gender, or other distinctions, like location, income, etc.

Market-based pricing: setting a price based on the value of the product in the perception of the customer.

Market share: the proportion of the total market value of a product or group of products or services that a company, service, or product holds. Market share is shown as a percentage of the total value or output of a market. The product, service, or company with a dominant market share is referred to as the market leader.

Maslow's hierarchy of needs theory: Maslow stated that people are motivated to achieve certain needs. When one need is fulfilled a person seeks to fulfill the next one, and so on. The theory is that one cannot effectively move to the next level without satisfying the previous level. So, if one's basic needs are not met, they cannot feel safe for example. The Maslow's hierarchy of needs are as such:

1. *Biological and Physiological needs* - air, food, drink, shelter, warmth, sex, sleep.
2. *Safety needs* - protection from elements, security, order, law, stability, freedom from fear.
3. *Social needs* - belongingness, affection and love from others
4. *Esteem needs* - achievement, mastery, independence, status, dominance, prestige, self-respect, respect from others.
5. *Self-Actualization needs* - realizing personal potential, self-fulfillment, seeking personal growth and peak experiences.

Applying Maslow to business	
Maslow's hierarchy	**Business examples**
Step 5 - Self-actualization	Opportunities for creativity and personal growth, promotion
Step 4 - Esteem needs	Fancy job title, recognition of achievements
Step 3 - Social needs	Good team atmosphere, friendly supervision
Step 2 - Safety needs	Safe working conditions, job security
Step 1 - Physiological needs	Salary, decent working environment

http://www.bbc.com/news/magazine-23902918

Matrix management: a technique of managing an organization (or, more commonly, part of an organization) through a series of dual-reporting relationships instead of a more traditional linear management structure.

Matrix organizational structure: an organizational structure that facilitates the horizontal flow of skills and information and the main idea is that the management of large projects or product developments processes, drawing employees from different functional disciplines for assignment to a team without removing them from their respective positions.

Merchandizing: a branch of marketing theory and practice concerned with maximizing product sales by designing, packaging, pricing, and displaying goods in a way that stimulates higher sales volume. The underlying assumption in merchandising is that consumers may have a general need for (or interest in) a certain class of product, and it is the merchandiser's task to present the product in a way that best captures consumers' attention and persuades them that the product will fulfill their needs and wants.

Merit pay: an approach to compensation that rewards the higher performing employees with additional pay or incentive pay. Unlike profit sharing or similar bonus pay schemes, merit pay allows an employer to differentiate between the performance of the company as a whole and the performance of an individual.

Methods study: subjecting each part of a given piece of work to close analysis to eliminate every unnecessary element or operation, as a means of approaching the quickest and best method of performing the work. It also includes formulation of incentive schemes, and improvement and standardization of equipment, methods, operator training, working conditions, etc. Also called methods engineering.

Middle office: staff who do not interact directly with customers but are involved in making business decisions. Risk management is an example of a middle office function.

Management Information System (MIS): methods of using technology to help organizations better manage people and make decisions. The five primary components: 1) Hardware, 2) Software, 3) Data *(information for decision making),* 4) Procedures (design, development and documentation), and 5) People (individuals, groups, or organizations).

Mission statement: formal written pronouncements of the core purpose of a business. A good mission statement should address the aim and purpose of the company while mentioning important contributors, and defining the company's responsibilities to them. Visit www.missionstatements.com to review established mission statements to get an idea of how these are stated.

N

Nester: in advertising or marketing, a consumer who is not influenced by advertising hype but prefers value for money and traditional products.

Net asset value: the value of a company's stock assessed by subtracting any liabilities from the market value.

Net asset value per share: the value of a company's stock assessed by subtracting any liabilities from the market value and dividing the remainder by the number of shares of stock issued.

Net investment: an increase in the total capital invested. It is calculated as gross capital invested less an estimated figure for capital consumption or depreciation.

Net present value (NPV): the difference between the present value of cash inflows and the present value of cash outflows. NPV is used in capital budgeting to analyze the profitability of an investment or project.

Net price: the price paid for goods or services after all relevant discounts have been deducted.

Network management: top-level administration and maintenance of large networks, often in areas such as computers or telecommunications, but not including user terminal equipment. It often involves functions such as security, monitoring, control, allocation, deployment, coordination, and planning.

Network marketing: the selling of goods or services through a network of self-employed agents or representatives. Network marketing usually involves several levels of agents, each level on a different commission rate. Each agent is encouraged to recruit other agents.

Network organization: where long-term corporate partners supply goods and services to and through a central hub firm. Together, a network of small companies can present the appearance of a large corporation.

O

Obsolescence: in marketing, the decline of products in a market due to the introduction of better competitor products or rapid technology developments. Obsolescence of products can be a planned process, controlled by introducing deliberate minor cosmetic changes to a product every few years to encourage new purchases. It can also be unplanned, however, and in some sectors the pace of technological change is so rapid that the rate of obsolescence is high. Obsolescence is part of the product life cycle, and if a product cannot be turned around, it may lead to product abandonment. In finance, the loss of value of a fixed asset due to advances in technology or changes in market conditions

Offshoring: the relocation by a company of a business process from one country to another—typically an operational process, such as manufacturing, or supporting processes, such as accounting or customer relations.

Oligarchy: an organization in which a small group of managers exercises control. Within an oligarchy, the controlling group often directs the organization for its own purposes, or for purposes other than the best interests of the organization.

Operating cost: expenses associated with administering a business on a day to day basis. Operating costs include both fixed costs and variable costs. Fixed costs, such as overhead, remain the same regardless of the number of products produced; variable costs, such as materials, can vary according to how much product is produced.

Opportunity cost: the cost of passing up the next best choice when making a decision. For example, if an asset such as capital is used for one purpose, the opportunity cost is the value of the next best purpose the asset could have been used for. Opportunity cost analysis is an important part of a company's decision-making processes, but is not treated as an actual cost in any financial statement.

Overall rate of return: the aggregate of all the dividends received over an investment's life together with its capital gain or loss at the date of its realization, calculated either before or after tax. It is one of the ways an investor can look at the performance of an investment.

P

Panel study: study that provides longitudinal data on a group of people, households, employers, or other social unit, termed 'the panel', about whom information is collected over a period of months, years, or decades.

Payout ratio: also known as dividend payout ratio, the proportion of earnings paid out as dividends to shareholders, typically expressed as a percentage. The payout ratio can also be expressed as dividends paid out as a proportion of cash flow. The payout ratio is a key financial metric used to determine the sustainability of a company's dividend payments. A lower payout ratio is generally preferable to a higher payout ratio, with a ratio greater than 100% indicating the company is paying out more in dividends than it makes in net income.

The Payout ratio is calculated as follows:

Payout Ratio = Dividends per Share (DPS) / Earnings per Share (EPS)

P/E: the price of a security per share at a given time divided by its annual earnings per share. Often, the earnings used are trailing 12 month earnings, but some analysts use other forms. The P/E ratio is a way to help determine a security's stock valuation, that is, the fair value of a stock in a perfect market. It is also a measure of expected, but not realized, growth. Companies expected to announce higher earnings usually have a higher P/E ratio, while companies expected to announce lower earnings usually have a lower P/E ratio.

Personal brand: the public expression and projection of a person's identity, personality, values, skills, and abilities. It aims to influence the perceptions of others, emphasizing personal strengths and differentiating the individual from others.

PEST analysis: systems (see below) that should be considered when planning a business as these can have impacts on business success or failure:

> **P**: Political
> **E**: Economic
> **S**: Social
> **T**: Technical

(see also **STEEPLE analysis**).

Price differentiation: pricing strategy in which a company sells the same product at different prices in different markets.

Price learning ratio: a pricing strategy in which a company sells the same product at different prices in different markets.

Price to books ratio: the ratio of the value of all of a company's stock to its book value.

Primary data: is original research *conducted by you* (or someone hired) to collect data specifically for your current objective. You might conduct a survey, run an interview or a focus group, observe behavior, or do an experiment. You are going to be the person who obtains this raw data directly and it will be collected specifically for your current research need, unlike secondary data (see also **secondary data**).

Product abandonment: the ending of the manufacture and sale of a product. Products are abandoned for many reasons. The market may be saturated or declining, the product may be superseded by another, costs of production may become too high, or a product may simply become unprofitable. Product abandonment usually occurs during the decline phase of the product life cycle.

Product concept: the notion that the integrity of the product supersedes all other considerations and that quality alone determines the fate of the product. Therefore, no substantive marketing effort is required. A limit in this approach is that potential customers may not even be aware of the product's existence, much less be able to evaluate it for purchase.

Product life cycle: the product life cycle has 4 very clearly defined stages, each with its own characteristics that mean different things for business that are trying to manage the life cycle of their particular products:

Introduction Stage – this stage of the cycle could be the most expensive for a company launching a new product. The size of the market for the product is small, which means sales are low, although they will be increasing. On the other hand, the cost of things like research and development, consumer testing, and the marketing needed to launch the product can be very high, especially if it's a competitive sector.

Growth Stage – the growth stage is typically characterized by a strong growth in sales and profits, and because the company can start to benefit from economies of scale in production, the profit margins, as well as the overall amount of profit, will increase. This makes it possible for businesses to invest more money in the promotional activity to maximize the potential of this growth stage.

Maturity Stage – during the maturity stage, the product is established and the aim for the manufacturer is now to maintain the market share they have built up. This is probably the most competitive time for most products and businesses need to invest wisely in any marketing they undertake. They also need to consider any product modifications or improvements to the production process which might give them a competitive advantage.

Decline Stage – eventually, the market for a product will start to shrink, and this is what's known as the decline stage. This shrinkage could be due to the market becoming saturated (i.e. all the customers who will buy the product have already purchased it), or because the consumers are switching to a different type of product. While this decline may be inevitable, it may still be possible for companies to make some profit by switching to less-expensive production methods and cheaper markets.

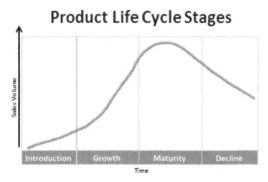

http://productlifecyclestages.com/product-life-cycle-examples/

Product mix: refers to the total number of product lines that a company offers to its customers. For example, a small company may sell multiple lines of products. Sometimes, these product lines are fairly similar, such as liquid soup and bar soap, which are used for cleaning and use similar technologies. Other times, the product lines are vastly different, such as over-the-counter cough medications and condiments (e.g. Reckitt Benckiser sells Mucinex and yellow mustard). The four dimensions to a company's product mix include width, length, depth and consistency.

Profit margin: net income divided by revenues, or net profits divided by sales. It measures how much out of every dollar of sales a company actually keeps in earnings. A higher profit margin indicates a more profitable company that has better control over its costs compared to its competitors. Profit margin is displayed as a percentage; a 20% profit margin, for example, means the company has a net income of $0.20 for each dollar of sales.

Pro-forma: a projection showing a business's likely financial statements after the completion of a planned transaction

Prospect theory: individuals make decisions that deviate from rational decision making by examining how the expected outcomes of alternative choices are perceived. The theory is based on the premise that people treat risks associated with perceived losses differently from risks associated with perceived gains. For example, if option A is a guaranteed win of $1,000, and option B is an 80 percent chance of winning $1,400 but a 20 percent chance of winning nothing, people tend to prefer option A.

Pull system:

> In manufacturing: production is based on actual daily demand (sales), and where information flows from market to management in a direction opposite to that in traditional (push) systems.

> In marketing: a pull strategy involves motivating customers to seek out your brand in an active process.

Push and pull strategy: promotional strategies to get product or service to market roughly divided into two separate camps (see **Pull system** and **Push system**).

Push system: a push promotional strategy involves taking the product directly to the customer via whatever means ensuring the customer is aware of your brand at the point of purchase.

Q

Qualitative research: qualitative models have generally been successful with short-term predictions, where the scope of the forecast is limited. Qualitative forecasts can be thought of as expert-driven, in that they depend on market mavens or the market as a whole to weigh in with an informed consensus. Qualitative models can be useful in predicting the short-term success of companies, products and services, but meets limitations due to its reliance on opinion over measurable data. Qualitative models include:

> *Market Research*: polling a large number of people on a specific product or service to predict how many people will buy or use it once launched.

> *Delphi Method*: asking field experts for general opinions and then compiling them into a forecast.

Quantitative research: quantitative forecasting methods are used when historical data on variables of interest are available—these methods are based on an analysis of historical data concerning the time series of the specific variable of interest and possibly other related time series. There are two major categories of quantitative forecasting methods. The first type uses the past trend of a particular variable to base the future forecast of the variable. As this category of forecasting methods simply uses time series on past data of the variable that is being forecasted, these techniques are called time series methods. The second category of quantitative forecasting techniques also uses historical data. But in forecasting future values of a variable, the forecaster examines the cause-and-effect relationships of the variable with other relevant variables such as the level of consumer confidence, changes in consumers' disposable incomes, the interest rate at which consumers can finance their spending through borrowing, and the state of the economy represented by such variables as the unemployment rate. Thus, this category of forecasting techniques uses past time series on many relevant variables to produce the forecast for the variable of interest. Forecasting techniques falling under this category are called causal methods, as the basis of such forecasting is the cause-and-effect relationship between the variable forecasted and other time series selected to help in generating the forecasts (see also **Forecasting**).

R

Ratio of net income after taxes to average owner's equity: net income divided by average owner's equity.

Rebadge: when one company buys a product or service from another company and sells it as part of their own product range.

Repositioning: a marketing strategy that changes aspects of a product or brand in order to change market position and alter consumer perceptions

Return on investment (ROI): the percentage return on a particular investment

S

Sampling: process of selecting units (e.g., people, organizations) from a population of interest so that by studying the sample we may fairly generalize the results back to the population from which they were chosen.

U.S. Securities and Exchange Commission (SEC): agency established to protect investors; to maintain fair, orderly, and efficient markets; and facilitate capital formation.

Secondary data: involves searching for *existing data* that was originally *collected by someone else.* You might look in journals, libraries, or go to online sources like the US census. You will apply what you find to your personal research problem, but the data you are finding was not originally collected by you, nor was it obtained for the exact purpose you are using it for. It is cheaper to use secondary data vs primary data because you do not bear the costs needed for research (see also **primary data**).

Selling concept: is predicated upon the notion that consumers will not make purchases in the absence of strong selling and promotional efforts.

Selling cost variance: the difference in expected revenue and actual revenue when the price of a unit changes. For example, if a company produced 1,000 units of a good and expected to sell them for $100/unit, it expected revenues of $100,000. If the actual price that the goods were sold at is $110, the company sees a selling price variance of $10,000 (1,000 units x $110/unit - $100,000).

Semi-variable cost: the amount of money paid to produce a product, which increases, though less than proportionally, with the quantity of the product made.

Shareholder: one who owns shares of stock in a corporation or mutual fund. For corporations, along with the ownership comes a right to declared dividends and the right to vote on certain company matters, including the board of directors

Stocks:

Common: carries the right to vote for the directors of the firm, but earns dividends only after dividends have been paid to the owners of preferred stock.

Preferred: has a claim on the firm's earnings before dividends may be paid on common stock and that has a prior claim on the corporation's assets in the event of liquidation. However, preferred stock usually has no voting rights.

STEEPLE analysis: expanded from PEST analysis, these systems should be considered when planning business as these can have impacts on business success or failure: Social, technological, environmental, economic, political, legislative, ethical (see also **PEST analysis**).

Stress test: a risk management tool that helps to identify how vulnerable a business, portfolio, or venture might be to unusual, negative circumstances. It may involve scenario analysis or simulation, based on hypothetical or historical data.

Supply chain management (SCM): the oversight of materials, information, and finances as they move in a process from supplier to manufacturer to wholesaler to retailer to consumer. Supply chain management involves coordinating and integrating these flows both within and among companies. It is said that the ultimate goal of any effective supply chain management system is to reduce inventory (with the assumption that products are available when needed).

Survey: the collection of data from a given population for the purpose of analysis of a particular issue. Data is often collected from only a sample of a population, and this is known as a sample survey. Surveys are used widely in research, especially in market research.

Sustainable advantage: a competitive advantage that can be maintained over the long term, as opposed to one resulting from a short-term tactical promotion

SWOT analysis: a tool that identifies the **s**trengths, **w**eaknesses, **o**pportunities and **t**hreats of an organization. Specifically, SWOT is a basic, straightforward model that assesses what an organization can and cannot do as well as its potential opportunities and threats. The method of SWOT analysis is to take the information from an environmental analysis and separate it into internal (strengths and weaknesses) and external issues (opportunities and threats). Once this is completed, SWOT analysis determines what may assist the firm in accomplishing its objectives, and what obstacles must be overcome or minimized to achieve desired results.

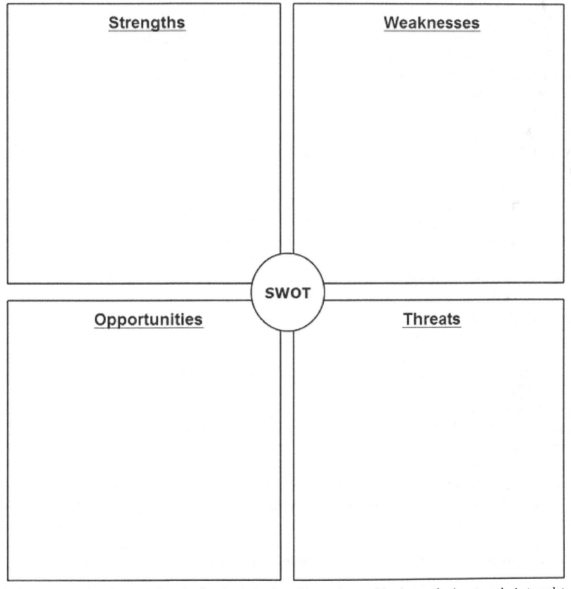

Blank SWOT template for quick download and printing http://creately.com/blog/examples/swot-analysis-templates-creately/#SwotTemplatePrinting

T

Tertiary industry: segment of the economy that provides services to its consumers. This includes a wide range of businesses including financial institutions, schools, transports and restaurants.

Terotechnology: a multidisciplinary technique that combines the areas of management, finance, and engineering with the goal of optimizing life-cycle costs for physical assets and technologies. Terotechnology is concerned with acquiring and caring for physical assets. It covers the specification and design.

Theory of constraints: a management paradigm that views any manageable system as being limited in achieving more of its goals by a very small number of constraints. There is always at least one constraint. The underlying premise of theory of constraints is that organizations can be measured and controlled by variations on three measures: throughput, operational expense, and inventory. Throughput is the rate at which the system generates money through sales. Inventory is all the money that the system has invested in purchasing things which it intends to sell. Operational expense is all the money the system spends in order to turn inventory into throughput

Theory X and Y: theory X represents a negative view of human nature that assumes individuals generally dislike work, are irresponsible, and require close supervision to do their jobs. Theory Y denotes a positive view of human nature and assumes individuals are generally industrious, creative, and able to assume responsibility and exercise self-control in their jobs. One would expect then, that managers holding assumptions about human nature that are consistent with Theory X might exhibit a managerial style that is quite different than managers who hold assumptions consistent with Theory Y.

Theta: a measure of the rate of decline in the value of an option due to the passage of time. Theta can also be referred to as the time decay on the value of an option. If everything is held constant, then the option will lose value as time moves closer to the maturity of the option.

Top down approach: an autocratic style of leadership in which strategies and solutions are identified by senior management and then cascaded down through an organization. The top-down approach can be considered a feature of large bureaucracies. A number of management gurus have criticized it as an out-of-date style that leads to stagnation and business failure.

Total return: Total return is one more way to evaluate investment decisions, and because it totals all factors it is perhaps a calculation that investors value most—or should.

Treasury bond: a bond issued by the US government that bears fixed interest.

Turnaround management: uses analysis and planning to save troubled companies and returns them to solvency. Turnaround management involves management review, activity based costing, root failure causes analysis, and SWOT analysis to determine why the company is failing.

V

Value added: the enhancement added to a product or service by a company before the product is offered to customers.

Value analysis: a cost reduction and problem-solving technique that analyzes an existing product or service in order to reduce or eliminate any costs that do not contribute to value or performance. Value analysis usually focuses on design issues relating to the function of a product or service, looking at the properties that make it work, or which are USPs.

Value chain: sequence of business functions in which customer usefulness is added to products. The general six primary functions are: research and development (R&D), design of products and processed, production, marketing, distribution, and customer service (See also **competitive advantage**).

According to Michael E. Porter the value chain should be grouped into two main groups of activities: *primary activities* and *support activities*. Primary activities are directly concerned with the production or delivery of certain products or services. Support activities help to support the efficiency and effectiveness of primary activities.

Primary Activities

> Inbound logistics
> Operations
> Outbound logistics
> Marketing and sales
> Service

Support activities

Procurement
Technology development
Human resource management
Firm infrastructure

Value-in-use analysis: in purchasing the examination of each procurement item to ascertain its total cost of acquisition, maintenance, and usage over its useful life and, wherever feasible, to replace it with a more cost effective substitute.

Variable costs: a cost of labor, material or overhead that changes according to the change in the volume of production units. Combined with fixed costs, variable costs make up the total cost of production. While the total variable cost changes with increased production, the total fixed costs stays the same.

Vertical integration: the process in which several steps in the production and/or distribution of a product or service are controlled by a single company or entity, in order to increase that company's or entity's power in the marketplace. For example, a farmer who launches his own food brand and grocery store. This was the case with one such famer in the UK who formed the Nutriva Group whereas in 2009 sales reached $5 million, nearly doubling in subsequent years.

W

Work sampling: the statistical technique for determining the proportion of time spent by workers in various defined categories of activity (e.g. setting up a machine, assembling two parts, idle time...etc.)

World Trade Organization (WTO): an international organization set up with the goal of reducing restrictions in trade between countries.

Write-down value: the value of an asset after accounting for depreciation or amortization. Written-down value is also called book value or net book value. It is calculated by subtracting accumulated depreciation or amortization from the asset's original value. Written-down value reflects the asset's present worth from an accounting perspective. An asset's written-down value will appear on the company's balance sheet.

X, Y, Z

Yield: the income return on an investment. This refers to the interest or dividends received from a security and is usually expressed annually as a percentage based on the investment's cost, its current market value or its face value.

Zero-budgeting: method where cash flow budgets and operating plans each fiscal period must start from scratch with no pre-authorized funds. A zero-based budget is one where total income minus total expenses should equal $0. This method forces the company to assign every dollar of income to an expense.

Chapter 3

Key Ratios in Business Management

Key Ratios in Business Management

Asset utilization ratios

Accumulated depreciation to fixed assets ratio:

$$\frac{\text{Accumulated depreciation}}{\text{Total fixed assets}}$$

Break-even point:

$$\frac{\text{Total operating expenses}}{\text{Average gross margin percentage}}$$

$$\frac{\text{Total operating expenses} - (\text{Depreciation} + \text{Amortization} - \text{Other noncash expenses})}{\text{Average gross margin percentage}}$$

Discretionary cost ratio:

$$\frac{\text{Discretionary costs}}{\text{Sales}}$$

Foreign exchange ratios:

$$\frac{\text{Foreign currency gains and losses}}{\text{Net income}}$$

$$\frac{\text{Foreign currency gains and losses}}{\text{Total sales}}$$

Fringe benefits to wages and salaries expense:

$$\frac{\text{Life insurance} + \text{Medical insurance} + \text{Pension funding expense} + \text{Other benefits}}{\text{Wages} + \text{Salaries} + \text{Payroll taxes}}$$

Goodwill to assets ratio:

$$\frac{\text{Unamortized goodwill}}{\text{Total assets}}$$

Interest expense to debt ratio:

$$\frac{\text{Interest expense}}{(\text{Short} - \text{term debt}) + (\text{Long} - \text{term debt})}$$

Investment turnover:

$$\frac{\text{Sales}}{\text{Stockholders' equity} + \text{Long} - \text{term liabilities}}$$

Margin of safety:

$$\frac{\text{Current sales level} - \text{Break} - \text{even point}}{\text{Current sales level}}$$

Net Present Value (NPV):

$$NPV = \sum_{t=1}^{T} \frac{C_t}{(1+r)^t} - C_0$$

where:

C_t = net cash inflow during the period

C_0 = initial investment

r = discount rate, and

t = number of time periods

Overhead rate:

$$\frac{\text{Total overhead expense}}{\text{Direct labor}}$$

$$\frac{\text{Total overhead expense}}{\text{Total machine hours}}$$

Overhead to cost of sales ratio:

$$\frac{\text{Total overhead expenses}}{\text{Cost of goods sold}}$$

$$\frac{\text{Total overhead expenses}}{\text{Direct materials} + \text{direct lab}}$$

$$\frac{\text{Total overhead expense}}{\text{Direct materials}}$$

Repairs and maintenance expense to fixed assets ratio:

$$\frac{\text{Total repairs and maintenance expense}}{\text{Total fixed assets before depreciation}}$$

Sales backlog ratio:

$$\frac{\text{Backlog of orders received}}{\text{Sales}}$$

$$\frac{\text{Total backlog}}{\text{Annual sales / days}}$$

Sales expenses to sales ratio:

$$\frac{\text{Sales salaries} + \text{Commissions} + \text{Sales travel expenses} + \text{Other sales expenses}}{\text{Sales}}$$

Sales per person:

$$\frac{\text{Annualized revenue}}{\text{Total full} - \text{time equivalents}}$$

Sales returns to gross sales ratio:

$$\frac{\text{Total sales returns}}{\text{Gross sales}}$$

Sales to administrative expenses ratio:

$$\frac{\text{Annualized net sales}}{\text{Total general and administrative expenses}}$$

Sales to equity ratio:

$$\frac{\text{Annual net sales}}{\text{Total equity}}$$

Sales to fixed assets ratio:

$$\frac{\text{Annualized net sales}}{\text{Total fixed assets}}$$

$$\frac{\text{Annualized net sales}}{\text{Total fixed assets prior to accumulated deprecitation}}$$

Sales to working capital ratio:

$$\frac{\text{Annualized net sales}}{(\text{Accounts receivable} + \text{Inventory} - \text{Accounts payable})}$$

Tax rate percentage:

$$\frac{\text{Income tax paid}}{\text{Before} - \text{tax income}}$$

$$\frac{\text{Income tax expense}}{\text{Before} - \text{tax income}}$$

Operating Performance Measurements

Core growth rate:

$$\frac{((\text{Current annual revenue} - \text{Annual revenue 5 years ago} - \text{Acquired revenue} - \text{Revenue recognition changes}))/(\text{Annual revenue 5 years ago})}{5} - \text{Average annual price increase}$$

Core operating earnings:

+ Employee stock option expenses
+ Restructuring charges from ongoing operations
+ Pension fund costs
+ Purchased R&D expenses
+ Asset write-downs
- Goodwill impairment charges
- Gains/losses from the sale of assets
- Pension gains
- Merger and acquisition-related expenses
- Litigation and insurance settlement costs and proceeds
- Unrealized gains from hedging activities

Gross profit index:

$$\frac{\dfrac{\text{Gross profit in period two}}{\text{Sales in period two}}}{\dfrac{\text{Gross profit in period one}}{\text{Sales in period one}}}$$

Gross profit percentage:

$$\frac{\text{Revenue} - (\text{Overhead} + \text{Direct materials} + \text{Direct labor})}{\text{Revenue}}$$

$$\frac{\text{Revenue} - \text{Direct materials}}{\text{Revenue}}$$

Investment income percentage:

$$\frac{\text{Dividend income} + \text{Interest income}}{\text{Carrying value of investments}}$$

Net income percentage:

$$\frac{\text{Net income}}{\text{Revenue}}$$

Operating assets ratio:

$$\frac{\text{Assets used to create revenue}}{\text{Total assets}}$$

Operating leverage ratio:

$$\frac{\text{Sales} - \text{Variable expenses}}{\text{Operating income}}$$

Operating profit percentage:

$$\frac{\text{Sales} - (\text{Cost of good sold} + \text{Sales, general, and administrative expenses})}{\text{Sales}}$$

Profit per customer visit:

$$\frac{\text{Net profits}}{\text{Total customer visits}}$$

Profit per person:

$$\frac{\text{Net profit}}{\text{Total full} - \text{time equivalents}}$$

Quality of earnings ratio:

$$\frac{\text{Earnings} - \text{Cash from operations}}{(\text{Beginning assets}) + (\text{Ending assets})/2}$$

Sales margin:

$$\frac{\text{Gross margin} - \text{Sales expenses}}{\text{Gross sales}}$$

Sales to operating income ratio:

$$\frac{\text{Operating income}}{(\text{Net sales }) - (\text{Investment income})}$$

Cash Flow Measurements

Cash flow coverage ratio:

$$\frac{\text{Total debt payments} + \text{Dividend payments} + \text{Capital expenditures}}{\text{Net income} + \text{Noncash expenses} - \text{Noncash sales}}$$

Cash flow from operations:

$$\frac{\text{Income from operations} + \text{Noncash expenses} - \text{Noncash sales}}{\text{Income from operations}}$$

$$\frac{\text{Net income} + \text{Noncash expenses} - \text{Noncash sales}}{\text{Net income}}$$

Cash flow return on assets:

$$\frac{\text{Net income} + \text{Noncash expenses} - \text{Noncash sales}}{\text{Total assets}}$$

Cash flow return on sales:

$$\frac{\text{Net income} + \text{Noncash expenses} - \text{Noncash sales}}{\text{Total sales}}$$

Cash flow to debt ratio:

$$\frac{\text{Net income} + \text{Noncash expenses} - \text{Noncash sales}}{\text{Debt} + \text{Lease obligations}}$$

$$\frac{\text{Net income} + \text{Noncash expenses} - \text{Noncash sales}}{\text{Total long} - \text{term debt payments for the period}}$$

Cash flow to fixed asset requirements:

$$\frac{\text{Net income} + \text{Noncash expenses} - \text{Noncash sales}}{\text{Budgeted fixed asset purchases}}$$

$$\frac{\text{Net income} + \text{Noncash expenses} - \text{Noncash sales} - \text{Dividends} - \text{Principal payments}}{\text{Budgeted fixed asset purchases}}$$

Cash receipts to billed sales and progress payments:

$$\frac{\text{Cash receipts}}{\text{Billed sales} + \text{Billed progress payments}}$$

Cash reinvestment ratio:

$$\frac{\text{Increase in fixed assets} + \text{Increase in working capital}}{\text{Net income} + \text{Noncash expenses} - \text{Noncash sales} - \text{Dividends}}$$

Cash to current assets ratio:

$$\frac{\text{Cash} + \text{Short} - \text{term marketable securities}}{\text{Current assets}}$$

Cash to current liabilities ratio:

$$\frac{\text{Cash} + \text{short} - \text{term marketable securities}}{\text{Current liabilities}}$$

Cash to working capital ratio:

$$\frac{\text{Cash} + \text{Short} - \text{term marketable securities}}{\text{Current asset} - \text{Current liabilities}}$$

Dividend payout ratio:

$$\frac{\text{Total dividend payments}}{\text{Net income} + \text{Noncash expenses} - \text{Noncash sales}}$$

Expense coverage days:

$$\frac{\text{Cash} + \text{Short} - \text{term marketable securities} + \text{Accounts receivable}}{\text{Annual cash expenditures}/360}$$

Fixed charge coverage:

$$\frac{\text{Fixed expenses} + \text{Fixed payments}}{\text{Cash flow from operations}}$$

Stock price to cash flow ratio:

$$\frac{(\text{Stock price}) \times (\text{Number of shares oustanding})}{\text{Earnings before interest, taxes, depreciation and amortization}}$$

Liquidity Measurements

Accounts payable days:

$$\frac{\text{Accounts payable}}{\text{Purchases}/365}$$

Accounts payable turnover:

$$\frac{\text{Total purchases}}{\text{Ending accounts payable balance}}$$

Accounts receivable collection period:

$$\frac{\text{Average accounts receivable}}{\text{Annual sales}/365}$$

Accounts receivable investment:

$$\frac{\text{Average days to payment}}{360 \text{ days}} \times$$

Annual credit sales x
(1 – Gross margin %) x
(Cost of capital)

Accounts receivable turnover:

$$\frac{\text{Annualized credit sales}}{\text{Average accounts receivable + Notes payable by customers}}$$

Altman's Z-score bankruptcy prediction formula:

(Operating income/Total Assets) x 3.3
+
(Sales/Total assets) x 0.999
+
(Market value of common
Stock + Preferred stock)/(Total
liabilities) x 0.6
+
(Working capital/Total assets) x 1.2
+
(Retained earnings/Total assets) x 1.4

Cash ratio:

$$\frac{\text{Cash} + \text{Short} - \text{term}\ \underline{\text{marketable securities}}}{\text{Current liabilities}}$$

Current liability ratio:

$$\frac{\text{Current liabilities}}{\text{Total liabilities}}$$

Current ratio:

$$\frac{\text{Current assets}}{\text{Current liabilities}}$$

Days delinquent sales outstanding:

$$\frac{365/\text{Annualized credit sales}\ \underline{\text{from delinquent accounts}}}{\text{Average delinquent}\ \text{accounts receivable}}$$

Days of working capital:

$$\frac{(\text{Accounts receivable} + \text{Inventory} - \text{Accounts payable})}{\text{Net sales}/365}$$

Days sales in receivables index:

$$\frac{\dfrac{\text{Accounts receivable in period two}}{\text{Sales in period two}}}{\dfrac{\text{Accounts receivable in period one}}{\text{Sales in period one}}}$$

Defensive interval ratio:

$$\frac{\text{Cash} + \text{Marketable securities} + \underline{\text{Accounts receivable}}}{\text{Expected daily}\ \text{operating expenses}}$$

Ending receivable balance:

$$\frac{\text{Average receivable collection period x Sales forecast for period}}{\text{Days in period}}$$

Inventory to sales ratio:

$$\frac{\text{Sales}}{\text{Inventory}}$$

Inventory to working capital ratio:

$$\frac{\text{Inventory}}{\text{Accounts receivable + Inventory} - \text{Accounts payable}}$$

Inventory turnover:

$$\frac{\text{Cost of goods sold}}{\text{Inventory}}$$

or,

$$365 / \frac{\text{Cost of goods sold}}{\text{Inventory}}$$

or,

$$\frac{\text{Direct materials}}{\text{Raw materials inventory}}$$

Liquidity index:

$$\frac{\text{(Accounts receivable x Days to liquidate)} + \text{(Inventory x Days to Liquidate)}}{\text{Accounts receivable + Inventory}}$$

Noncurrent assets to noncurrent liabilities ratio:

$$\frac{\text{Noncurrent assets}}{\text{Noncurrent liabilities}}$$

Quick ratio:

$$\frac{\text{Cash} + \text{Marketable securities} + \text{Accounts receivable}}{\text{Current liabilities}}$$

Required current liabilities to total current liabilities ratio:

$$\frac{\text{Current liabilities with required payment dates}}{\text{Total current liabilities}}$$

Risky asset conversion ratio:

$$\frac{\text{Cost of assets with minimal cash conversion value}}{\text{Total assets}}$$

Sales to current assets ratio:

$$\frac{\text{Sales}}{\text{Current assets}}$$

Short-term debt to long-term debt ratio:

$$\frac{\text{Total short} - \text{term debt}}{\text{Total long} - \text{term debt}}$$

Working capital productivity:

$$\frac{\text{Annual sales}}{\text{Working capital}}$$

Working capital to debt ratio:

$$\frac{\text{Cash} + \text{Accounts receivable} + \text{Inventory} - \text{Accounts payable}}{\text{Debt}}$$

Capital Structure and Solvency Measurements

Accruals to assets ratio:

$$\frac{\text{Change in working capital} - \text{Change in cash} - \text{Change in depreciation}}{\text{Change in total assets}}$$

Average quality index:

$$\frac{1 - \dfrac{\text{Current assets in period two} + \text{Net fixed assets in period two}}{\text{Total assets in period two}}}{1 - \dfrac{\text{Current assets in period one} + \text{Net fixed assets in period one}}{\text{Total assets in period one}}}$$

Debt coverage ratio:

$$\frac{\text{Earnings before interest and taxes}}{\text{Interest} + \dfrac{\text{Scheduled pricipal payments}}{(1 - \text{Tax rate})}}$$

Debt to equity ratio:

$$\frac{\text{Debt}}{\text{Equity}}$$

Funded capital ratio:

$$\frac{\text{Stockholders' equity} + \text{Long} - \text{term debt}}{\text{Fixed assets}}$$

Issued shares to authorized shares:

$$\frac{\text{Issued shares} + \text{Stock options} + \text{Stock warrants} + \text{Convertible securities}}{\text{Total authorized shares}}$$

Preferred stock to total stockholders' equity:

$$\frac{\text{Preferred stock}}{\text{Stockholders' equity}}$$

Retained earnings to stockholders' equity:

$$\frac{\text{Retained earnings}}{\text{Total stockholders' equity}}$$

Times interest earned:

$$\frac{\text{Average cash flow}}{\text{Average interest expense}}$$

Times preferred dividend earned:

$$\frac{\text{Net income}}{\text{Preferred dividend}}$$

Return on Investment (ROI) Measurements

Book value per share:

$$\frac{\text{Total equity} - \text{Cost to liquidate preferred stock}}{\text{Total number of common shares outstanding}}$$

Dividend payout ratio:

$$\frac{\text{Dividend per share}}{\text{Earnings per share}}$$

Dividend yield ratio:

$$\frac{\text{Dividend per share}}{\text{Market price per share}}$$

Earnings per share:

$$\frac{\text{Net income} - \text{Dividends on preferred stock}}{\text{Number of outstanding common shares} + \text{Common stock equivalents}}$$

Economic value added:

$$(\text{Net investment}) \times (\text{Actual return on investment} - \text{Percentage cost of capital})$$

Equity growth rate:

$$\frac{\text{Net income} - \text{Common stock dividends} - \text{Preferred stock dividends}}{\text{Beginning common stockholders' equity}}$$

Financial leverage index:

$$\frac{\text{Return on equity}}{\text{Return on assets}}$$

Net worth:

$$\frac{\text{Total assets} - \text{Total Liabilities} - \text{Preferred stock dividends}}{\text{Total outstanding common shares}}$$

Percentage change in earnings per share:

$$\frac{\text{Incremental change in earnings per share}}{\text{Earnings per share from previous period}}$$

Relative value of growth:

$$\frac{\dfrac{\text{Sustainable cash flow}}{(\text{Weighted average cost of capital}) - (\text{Investors' growth expectations}) - (1\%)}}{\dfrac{(\text{Current revenue}) \text{x } 1\% \text{ x } (1 - \text{Tax rate \%})}{(\text{Weighted average cost of capital}) - (\text{Investors' growth expectations})}}$$

Return on assets employed:

$$\frac{\text{Net profit}}{\text{Total assets}}$$

Return on common equity:

$$\frac{\text{Net income} - \text{Preferred stock dividends}}{\text{Common stockholders' equity}}$$

Return on equity percentage:

$$\frac{\text{Net income}}{\text{Total equity}}$$

Return on infrastructure employed:

$$\frac{\text{Before} - \text{tax earnings}}{\text{Information technology operating expenses}}$$

Return on operating assets:

$$\frac{\text{Net income}}{\text{Assets used to create revenue}}$$

Tangible book value:

Book value – (Goodwill + Other intangibles)

Market Performance Measurements

Capitalization rate:

$$\frac{\text{Earnings per share}}{\text{Market price per share}}$$

Cost of capital:

$$\frac{\begin{array}{c}\text{Interest expense x} \\ (1 - \text{Tax rate})\end{array}}{\begin{array}{c}\text{Amount of debt} - \text{Debt} \\ \text{acquisition fees} + \text{Premium} \\ \text{on debt} - \text{Discount on debt}\end{array}}$$
$$+$$
$$\frac{\text{Interest expense}}{\text{Amount of preferred stock}}$$
$$+$$
$$\text{Risk-free return} + (\text{Beta x} \\ (\text{Average stock return} - \\ \text{Risk-free return}))$$

Enterprise value/earnings ratio:

$$\frac{\begin{array}{c}(\text{Total shares x Stock price}) + \\ \text{Debt} - \text{Cash} - \text{Marketable} \\ \text{securities}\end{array}}{\text{Net income} - \text{Interest expense}}$$

Insider stock buy-sell ratio:

$$\frac{\begin{array}{c}\text{Number of stock sale} \\ \text{transactions by insiders}\end{array}}{\begin{array}{c}\text{Number of stock purchase} \\ \text{transactions by insiders}\end{array}}$$

Market value added:

(Number of common shares
outstanding x Share price) +
(Number of preferred shares
outstanding x Share price) –
(Book value of invested
capital)

Price/earnings ratio:

$$\frac{\text{Average common stock price}}{\text{Net income per share}}$$

Sales to stock price ratio:

$$\frac{\text{Annual net sales}}{\text{Average common stock price}}$$

Stock options to common shares ratio:

$$\frac{\text{Total stock options}}{\text{Total common shares outstanding}}$$

$$\frac{\text{Total vested stock options}}{\text{Total common shares outstanding}}$$

$$\frac{\text{Total vested options in the money}}{\text{Total common shares outstanding}}$$

Accounting/Finance Measurements

Average employee expense report turnaround time:

(Date of payment to
Employees) – (Date of expense
report receipt)

Average time to issue invoices:

$$\frac{\text{(Sum of invoice dates)} - \text{(Sum of shipment dates)}}{\text{Number of invoices issued}}$$

Bad debt percentage:

$$\frac{\text{Total bad debt dollars recognized}}{\text{Total outstanding accounts receivable}}$$

$$\frac{\text{Total bad debt dollars recognized}}{\text{Total credit sales}}$$

Borrowing base usage percentage:

$$\frac{\text{Amount of debt outstanding}}{(\text{Accounts receivable x Allowable percentage}) + (\text{Inventory x Allowable percentage})}$$

Brokerage fee percentage:

$$\frac{\text{Bank/broker transaction fees charged}}{\text{Total funds invested}}$$

$$\frac{\text{Bank/broker transaction fees charged}}{\text{Number of bank/broker transactions processed}}$$

Collection effectiveness index:

$$\frac{\text{Beginning receivables} + \text{Credit sales} - \text{Ending total receivables}}{\text{Beginning receivables} + \text{Credit sales} - \text{Ending current receivables}} \text{ x } 100$$

Cost of credit:

Discount %/(100 – Discount %) x (360/(Full allowed payment days – Discount days))

Earnings rate on invested funds:

$$\frac{\text{Interest earned} + \text{Increase in market value of securities}}{\text{Total funds invested}}$$

Internal audit efficiency:

$$\frac{\text{Number of internal audits completed}}{\text{Number of internal audits planned}}$$

Internal audit savings to cost percentage:

$$\frac{\text{Internal audit recommended savings}}{\text{Internal audit expense}}$$

Payroll transaction fees per employee:

$$\frac{\text{Total payroll outsourcing fee per payroll}}{\text{Total number of employees itemized in payroll}}$$

Percent of cash applied on day of receipt:

$$\frac{\text{Dollars of cash receipts applied on day of receipt}}{\text{Total dollars of incoming cash on day of receipt}}$$

Percent of receivables over XX days old:

$$\frac{\text{Dollar amount of outstanding receivables} > \text{XX days old}}{\text{Total dollars of outstanding receivables}}$$

Percentage collected of dollar volume assigned:

$$\frac{\text{Cash received from collection agency}}{\text{Total accounts receivable assigned to collection agency}}$$

Percentage of payment discounts missed:

$$\frac{\text{Number of payment discounts missed}}{\text{Total number of payment discounts available}}$$

Percentage of tax filing dates missed:

$$\frac{\text{Total number of tax returns filed late}}{\text{Total number of tax returns filed}}$$

Proportion of products costed prior to release:

$$\frac{\text{Number of products costed prior to release}}{\text{Total number of products released}}$$

Purchase discounts taken to total discounts:

$$\frac{\text{Total purchase discounts taken}}{\text{Total purchases}}$$

Time to produce financial statements:

Financial statement issue date – First day of the month

Transaction error rate:

$$\frac{\text{Number of errors}}{\text{Total number of transaction processed}}$$

Transactions processed per person:

$$\frac{\text{Total number of transactions processed}}{\text{Number of full} - \text{time equivalents required to complete transactions}}$$

Unmatched receipts exposure:

$$\frac{\text{Total balance in unmatched receipts suspense account}}{\text{Total accounts receivable balance}}$$

Engineering Department Measurements

Average number of distinct products per design platform:

$$\frac{\text{Total number of distinct products}}{\text{Total number of design platforms}}$$

Bill of material accuracy:

$$\frac{\text{Number of accurate parts listed in bill of materials}}{\text{Total of number of parts listed in bill of materials}}$$

Intangibility index:

$$\frac{\text{Total annual research and development expense}}{\text{Total annual capital spending}}$$

Labor routing accuracy:

$$\frac{\text{Number of correct machine times or machine codes}}{\text{Total number of routing line items}}$$

Percentage of existing parts reused in new products:

$$\frac{\text{Number of approved parts in bill of materials}}{\text{Total number of parts in bill of materials}}$$

Percentage of floor space utilization:

$$\frac{\text{Amount of floor space used for machinery, operator, and materials movement}}{\text{Total floor space}}$$

Percentage of new parts used in new products:

$$\frac{\text{Number of new parts in bill of materials}}{\text{Total number of parts in bill of materials}}$$

Percentage of new products introduced:

$$\frac{\text{Number of new products introduced in the period}}{\text{Number of products available at the beginning of the period}}$$

Percentage of products reaching market before competition:

$$\frac{\text{Number of products released before competition}}{\text{Total number of products released}}$$

$$\frac{\text{Number or products released on schedule}}{\text{Total number of products released}}$$

Percentage of sales from new products:

$$\frac{\text{Sales from new products}}{\text{Total sales}}$$

Ratio of actual to target cost:

$$\frac{\text{Total of actual product costs}}{\text{Total of target costs}}$$

Science linkage index:

$$\frac{\text{Total research paper references in issued patents}}{\text{Number of patents issued}}$$

Time from design inception to production:

(Completed design sign-off date) – (Design start date)

Warranty claims percentage:

$$\frac{\text{Total number of warranty claims received}}{\text{Total number of products sold}}$$

Human Resources Department Measurements

Average time to hire:

$$\frac{\text{Sum for all completed job searchers [Job application date} - \text{Job application date]}}{\text{Number of completed job searches}}$$

Employee turnover:

$$\frac{\text{Number of FTE employees who resigned}}{\text{(Total FTE employees at beginning of period} + \text{Total FTE employees at end of period)}/2}$$

Intern hiring rate:

$$\frac{\text{Number of intern job offers accepted}}{\text{Number of interns working for the company during the preceding year}}$$

Late personnel requisitions ratio:

$$\frac{\text{Number of personnel requisitions open more than XX days}}{\text{Number of personnel reuisitions opened during past three months}}$$

Ratio of support staff to total staff:

$$\frac{\text{(Beginning FTE support staff + Ending FTE support staff)/2}}{\text{(Beginning FTE employees + Ending FTE employees)/2}}$$

Logistics Department Measurements

Average time to ship:

(Delivery date) – (Date order was sent to shipping area)

Distribution turnover:

$$\frac{\text{Dollars of manufacturing purchases per year}}{\text{Dollar value of incoming inventory}}$$

Economic order quantity:

The root of ((2 x Total usage in units x Cost per order)/ Carrying cost per unit)

Economic production run size:

The root of ((2 x Total unit demand x Run setup cost)/ Carrying cost per unit)

EDI supplier percentage:

$$\frac{\text{Number of suppliers with EDI linkages}}{\text{Total number of suppliers}}$$

Finished goods inventory turns:

(Finished goods dollars consumed/Finished goods inventory dollars on hand) x 12

Freight audit recovery ratio:

$$\frac{\text{Total freight billings refund}}{\text{Total freight billings}}$$

Incoming components correct quantity percentage:

$$\frac{\text{Quantity of orders with correct parts quantity delivered}}{\text{Total quantity of orders delivered}}$$

Inventory accuracy:

$$\frac{\text{Number of accurate test items}}{\text{Total number of items sampled}}$$

Number of orders to place in a period:

$$\frac{\text{Total usage in units}}{\text{Economic order quantity}}$$

Obsolete inventory percentage:

$$\frac{\text{Cost of inventory items with no recent usage}}{\text{Total inventory cost}}$$

On-time delivery percentage:

Required delivery date –
Actual delivery date

On-time parts delivery percentage:

(Actual arrival date) –
(Requested arrival date)

Order fill rate:

$$\frac{\text{Number of customer orders completely filled by promised ship date}}{\text{Number of customer orders having promised ship dates within the measurement period}}$$

Percentage of actual payments varying from purchase order price:

$$\frac{\text{Dollar total of excess costs over purchase order costs}}{\text{Total of all purchase order costs}}$$

Percentage of certified suppliers:

$$\frac{\text{Number of certified production suppliers}}{\text{Total number of production suppliers}}$$

Percentage of inventory > XX days old:

$$\frac{\text{Dollars of inventory > XX days old}}{\text{Total dollar of inventory}}$$

Percentage of products damaged in transit:

$$\frac{\text{Damage} - \text{related customer complaints}}{\text{Number of orders shipped}}$$

Percentage of purchase orders issued below minimum dollar level:

$$\frac{\text{Number of purchase orders issued below minimum dollar level}}{\text{Total number of purchase orders issued}}$$

Percentage of receipts authorized by purchase orders:

$$\frac{\text{Receipt line items authorized by open purchase orders}}{\text{Total receipt line items}}$$

Percentage of returnable inventory:

$$\frac{\text{Dollars of returnable inventory}}{\text{Total dollars of inventory}}$$

Percentage of sales through distributors:

$$\frac{\text{Total dollars of sales to distributors}}{\text{Total dollars of sales}}$$

Picking accuracy for assembled products:

$$100\% - \frac{\text{Number of quantity errors} + \text{Number of part errors}}{\text{Total number of product kits sampled}}$$

Production schedule accuracy:

$$\frac{\text{Number of scheduled jobs completed}}{\text{Number of jobs scheduled for completion}}$$

Proportion of corporate credit card usage:

$$\frac{\text{Number of credit card purchase transactions}}{\text{Total number of purchase transactions}}$$

Purchased component defect rate:

$$\frac{\text{Number of rejected components}}{\text{Total number of components received}}$$

Raw material content:

$$\frac{\text{Raw material dollars sold}}{\text{Sales}}$$

Raw material inventory turns:

$$(\text{Raw material dollars consumed}/\text{Raw material inventory dollars on hand}) \times 12$$

Production Measurements

Acceptable product completion percentage:

$$\frac{(\text{Number of products in production run}) - (\text{Number of rejected products})}{\text{Number of products in production run}}$$

Average equipment setup time:

$$(\text{Start time for new production run}) - (\text{Stop time for last production run})$$

Break-even plant capacity:

$$\frac{\text{Current utilization level x total fixed costs}}{\text{Sales} - \text{Variable expenses}}$$

Constraint productivity:

$$\frac{\text{Number of units produced per hour}}{\text{Number of hours worked}}$$

Constraint rework percentage:

$$\frac{\text{Rework hours used in constraint operation}}{\text{Total hours of constraint}}$$

Constraint schedule attainment:

$$\frac{\text{Part hours produced} + \text{Rework hours} - \text{Reduction in actual hours from standard}}{\text{Part hours scheduled}}$$

Constraint utilization:

$$\frac{\text{Actual hours used in constraint operation}}{\text{Total constraint hours available}}$$

Degree of unbalance:

$$\frac{\text{Maximum capacity of the work cell bottleneck operation}}{\text{Maximum capacity of the next most restrictive work cell operation}}$$

Indirect expense ratio:

$$\frac{\text{Indirect production cost in period two/Units produced in period two}}{\text{Indirect production cost in period one/Units produced in period one}}$$

Maintenance expense to fixed assets ratio:

$$\frac{\text{Maintenance and repair expense}}{\text{Total gross fixed assets}}$$

Manufacturing critical path time:

(Order receipt date and time) –
(Customer delivery date
and time)

Manufacturing effectiveness:

$$\frac{\text{Throughput hours shipped}}{\text{Constraint hours consumed}}$$

Manufacturing efficiency:

$$\frac{\text{Current cycle time}}{\text{Value} - \text{added time}}$$

Mean time between failures:

$$\frac{\text{Sum of ((stop time)} - \text{(start time))}}{\text{Total number of production runs measured}}$$

On-time delivery ratio:

$$\frac{\text{Number of orders shipped by due date}}{\text{Total number of orders shipped}}$$

Productivity index:

$$\frac{\text{Total change in output quantities}}{\text{Total change in input quantities}}$$

Reorder point:

(Average usage per time period x Lead time) + Safety stock

Scrap percentage:

$$\frac{\text{(Actual cost of goods sold)} - \text{(Standard cost of goods sold)}}{\text{Standard cost of goods sold}}$$

Takt time:

$$\frac{\text{Operating time}}{\text{Required quantity}}$$

Throughput effectiveness:

$$\frac{\text{Gross revenue} - \text{Variable expenses}}{\text{Operating expenses}}$$

Unit output per direct labor hour:

$$\frac{\text{Total units completed} + \text{Total unit equivalents} - \text{Total carryforward unit equivalents}}{\text{Total number of direct labor hours}}$$

Unscheduled machine downtime percentage:

$$\frac{\text{Total minutes of unscheduled downtime}}{\text{Total minutes of machine time}}$$

Warranty claims percentage:

$$\frac{\text{Total number of warranty claims received}}{\text{Total number of products sold}}$$

Work-in-progress turnover:

$$\frac{\text{Annual cost of goods sold}}{\text{Total work} - \text{in} - \text{progress}}$$

Sales and Marketing Measurements

Browse to buy conversion rate:

$$\frac{\text{Number of buying customers}}{\text{Number of browsing customers}}$$

Customer turnover:

$$\frac{\text{Total number of customers} - \text{Invoiced customers}}{\text{Total number of customers}}$$

Days of backlog:

$$\frac{\text{Dollar volume of sales backlog}}{\text{Average annual sales/365}}$$

Direct mail effectiveness ratio:

$$\frac{\text{Number of leads generated}}{\text{Number of direct mail pieces issued}}$$

$$\frac{\text{Gross profit on direct mail sales}}{\text{Total direct mail expense}}$$

Inbound telemarketing retention rate:

$$\frac{\text{Number of customer order cancellations reversed}}{\text{Number of initial customer order cancellations requested}}$$

Market share:

$$\frac{\text{Dollar volume of company shipments}}{\text{Dollar volume of industry shipments}}$$

Net promoter score:

$$\frac{\text{Number of customers giving score of 9 or 10 on } 10 - \text{point scale}}{\text{Number of customers giving score of 1 through 6 pm } 10 - \text{point scale}}$$

Product demand elasticity:

$$\frac{\text{Percentage change in quantity}}{\text{Percentage change in price}}$$

Proportion of completed sales to homepage views:

$$\frac{\text{Number of sales transactions through company Web site}}{(\text{Total page view of company home page}) - (\text{Total hits by search bots})}$$

Pull-through rate:

$$\frac{\text{Number of customers placing an order}}{\text{Number of customers with whom contact was initially made}}$$

Quote to close ratio:

$$\frac{\text{Dollar value of orders received}}{\text{Dollar value of quoted orders}}$$

Sales effectiveness:

$$\frac{\text{Gross revenue} - \text{Variable cost of goods sold}}{\text{Constrait time used}}$$

Sales per salesperson:

$$\frac{\text{Nonrecurring sales}}{\text{Number of FTE sales personnel}}$$

Sales productivity:

$$\frac{(\text{Gross nonrecurring revenue}) - (\text{Variable cost of sales})}{\text{Sales expense}}$$

Sales trend percentage:

$$\frac{(\text{Total sales in current period}) - (\text{Total sales in previous period})}{\text{Total sales in previous period}}$$

Chapter 4

Sample Test Questions

1. The main role of the U.S. Securities and Exchange Commission (SEC) is:

   (a) To track and report exchange rates
   (b) Investor protection and law enforcement
   (c) Issuing U.S. stocks and bonds
   (d) Informing citizens on how to invest

2. According to Human Resources (HR) expert Mark Huselid what tool best communicates key organizational objectives to the workforce:

   (a) HR Master Excel Spreadsheet
   (b) The Human Resource Metric
   (c) The HR Scorecard
   (d) The HR Organizational Chart

3. The most common form of variable pay is:

   (a) Performance Bonuses
   (b) Raises
   (c) Tax incentives
   (d) IRA Matching or Equity-based compensation

4. What is the best example of an external influence to the company's human resources:

   (a) Labor unions
   (b) Organizational structure
   (c) Business objectives
   (d) Industry trends

5. The best way an Employment Planning Service can assist a person seeking employment to learn about the job and to make informed decisions is to have the prospect:

   (a) Provide them with primary and secondary data for the industry
   (b) Have them participate in job simulation
   (c) Have them job shadow
   (d) Have them interview those actually doing the job

6. Ms Carol Jones of *ABC Forecasting Agency* wants to prioritize her workers training needs. What 3 perspectives (method of assessing) should she follow to help in this process:

   (a) Difficulty, Importance, and Frequency
   (b) Difficulty, Influence, and Frequency

(c) Degree of Certainty, Influx of needs, and Forecast of decisions
(d) Decision, Individual needs, and Frequency

7. The development in organizations to help boost the economic potential in a society and to help generate the tools necessary to fuel its capitalistic nature is an example of what business theory:

    (a) Systems Theory
    (b) Organizational Theory
    (c) Capitalism Theory
    (d) Economic Theory

8. The first line benefit for offshoring is:

    (a) Improvements in the quality of goods, materials, and services
    (b) Increased profits due to the ability to offer a larger selection of goods
    (c) Decreased labor costs
    (d) Improved "Green" conditions domestically

9. What percentage of ownership of a company abroad by a US multinational is referred to as direct foreign investment:

    (a) 5%
    (b) 10%
    (c) 25%
    (d) 50%

10. What economic theory explains why it is beneficial for two parties – whether they are countries, regions, or businesses, to trade their goods and services:

    (a) Economic Trade Theory
    (b) Theory of Comparative Advantage
    (c) Theory of Opportunity Cost
    (d) Keynesian Economic Theory

11. Trends in increased service-based economies often leads to:

    (a) Influx of migrant workers
    (b) Increased minimal wages
    (c) Decreases in college enrollments
    (d) More skilled talent moving abroad

12. Mr. Roberts contacts *Accenty International, Inc.* in order to get a job complete in minimum time and at a low cost without domestic labor involved. Mr. Roberts outsources the job to *Accenty* that subsequently outsources the work to a

company in a foreign county. What model is Mr. Roberts looking to in order to get the job done?

(a) Outsourcing Direct Model
(b) Offshoring Contracting Model
(c) Global Delivery Model
(d) International Trade Model

13. *Novo Nordisk* is a pharmaceuticals company headquartered in Denmark but has established divisions of subsidiaries in Italy, Mexico, Switzerland, the Netherlands, and the United States. *Novo Nordisk* is an example of what type of company?

(a) Foreign-Domestic Company
(b) International Trade Corporation
(c) Global Corporation
(d) Multinational

14. The primary function of the *World Trade Organization* is:

(a) To resolve disputes related to international trade
(b) To ensure that trade is balanced among free countries
(c) To ensure corporate responsibility compliance among trading countries
(d) To oversee the agreement of the Uruguagy Round of free trade talks

15. Mr. Rose completed the financial statement for his company and reported a net income of $2 million. However, he forgot to deducted the taxes and interest expenses so considering that everything else was done correctly the $2 million really represented:

(a) Total revenue
(b) Profits
(c) Sales
(d) Operating income

16. In the *Product Life Cycle*, what usually follows "product maturity":

(a) Saturation
(b) Growth
(c) Decline
(d) Abandonment

17. The shareholder's equity should read:

(a) Revenue - costs
(b) Profit - loss
(c) Assets - liabilities

(d) Profit - taxes

18. Assume that you are presented with an investment opportunity that would cost $3,800 in today's money. Further assume that you can reasonably expect to generate $1,000 in income per year for each of five years and that the prevailing cost of money or interest rate is 8%. The discount factors each year are: (Year 1: .926; Year 2: .857; Year 3: .794; Year 4: .735; and Year 5: .681). What would be the net present value (NPV), and should you accept the opportunity?

(a) $-1007, no
(b) $1007, yes
(c) $1200, yes
(d) $193, yes

19. In accounting, the premise of the *theory of constraints* is that organizations can be measured and controlled by 3 measures. What are those measures?

(a) Throughput, operational expense, and inventory
(b) Materials, production, and the supply chain
(c) Throughput, operational expense, and sales
(d) Materials, manufacturing, and production

20. Company A is trying to determine target annual operating and target operating income per unit of Provalue II respectively. Determine these figures based on the information provided below:

Invested capital: $96,000,000
Target rate of return on investment: 18%

(a) $16,900,000; $86.50
(b) $17,280,000; $86.40
(c) $17,310,000; $86.40
(d) $18,280,000; $88.50

21. Susan Roberton is managing partner of a new 60-room motel. She anticipates renting these rooms for 16,000 nights next year. All room are similar and will rent for the same price. Branch estimates the following operating costs for the next year:

Variable operating costs: $4 per room-night

Fixed costs:
        Salaries/wages $170,000
        Maintenance   48,000
        Other operating/admin costs   122,000

What are the total fixed costs?

(a) $340,000
(b) $404,000
(c) $170,000
(d) $214,000

22. What function is not one of the six primary functions of the *value chain*?

(a) Research and development (R&D)
(b) Design of products and processes
(c) Production
(d) Human resources

23. The *selling concept* is predicated upon the notion that consumers:

(a) Will make purchases in the absence of strong selling and promotional efforts
(b) Will be undecided about purchases without coupons or incentives
(c) Will not make purchases in the absence of strong selling and promotional efforts
(d) Will make purchases without promotions, but will likely return these products later

24. Mr. Alson wants to ask field experts for general opinions and then compile these into a forecast. What type of research method would Mr. Alson most likely use?

(a) Delphi Method
(b) Market research
(c) Polling
(d) Forecast research method

25. Mr. Jones has recently taken over as CEO of the Company C. At the helm Mr. Jones took on total authority and control over all decision-making. What type of leadership style is Mr. Jones likely aligned to?

(a) Democratic
(b) Collegial
(c) Demanding
(d) Autocratic

26. ABCD company has decided to dispose of an old machine. However, before doing so the manager wants to consider the tax consequence of disposing an old machine. What would be the tax savings on the loss of the machine given the following data?

Current disposal value of old machine $ 6,500

Deducted book value	40,000
Loss on disposal of machine	($33,500)

(a) 0
(b) $13,400
(c) $6,900
(d) -6,500

27. Calculate the foreign ROI in foreign currency for Peno's Inns in Mexico City based on the following information:

The investment (total assets) in Mexico City is 30,000,000 pesos. The operating income of Peno's Inn is 2011 was 6,000,000 pesos. What is the ROI, calculated using pesos?

(a) 18%
(b) 20%
(c) 25%
(d) 30%

28. Company A and Company B were told by the government that they were not allowed to merge because they would then be a monopoly. What laws are the government following?

(a) Anti-monopoly laws
(b) Merger protection laws
(c) Consumer protections laws
(d) Anti-trust laws

29. Expense occurred which gives benefit for less than twelve months is known as _____.

(a) Capital Expense
(b) Revenue Expense
(c) Revenue Receipt
(d) Deferred Expense

30. Price of common stock of Alaba Corp in market is $60 per share and purchase of each share gives the buyer a subscription right. If someone has four rights then an additional share of common stock can be purchased at a subscription price of $54 per share. What would be the approximate theoretical value of a right if the company is currently selling common stocks "rights-on"?

(a) $0.96
(b) $1.20

(c) $1.50
(d) $6.00

31. Using the information of the above question, what will be the approximate theoretic value of one share of Alaba Corp if it goes "ex-rights?"

(a) $58.80
(b) $57.50
(c) $56.80
(d) $59.04

32. The government of an Asian country insists that CPI is a measure of consumer prices rather than the measure of cost of living.   That is actually the best news for all.

Using information above it can be assumed that during a typical inflation:

(a) CPI rises by less than cost of living does
(b) CPI rises by more than cost of living does
(c) CPI and cost of living rise by same amount
(d) Rise in CPI and cost of living does not have any consistent relationship

33. If Labbot Pharmacy gets an invoice for the purchase with the date 10/21/12 subjected to credit terms "3/10, net 30 EOM" what is last possible date on which the payment has to be made:

        (i)   if the discount is taken?
        (ii)   if the discount is not taken?

(a) Nov 1 and Nov 20, respectively
(b) Nov 10 and Nov 20, respectively
(c) Nov 10 and Nov 30, respectively
(d) Dec 10 and Dec 30, respectively

34. For the previous estimate of $3.835 trillion, the Commerce Ministry revised the real GDP of the country to $3.877 trillion. Before any adjustment for inflation was made, the GDP was $4.603 trillion, up from $4.523 trillion. What is the GDP deflator used in the revision of the calculation?

(a) 118.0 or less
(b) Nnot greater than 118.5
(c) Greater than 118.5, but not greater than 119
(d) More than 119.0

35. Which of the following bond option provides most protection to the investor?

    (a) Debentures
    (b) First-mortgage bonds
    (c) Subordinated debentures
    (d) Income bonds

36. Consider the following information:

    Owner's Equity = $50,500
    Assets = $99,500.

    What will be the liabilities?

    (a) $49,000
    (b) $55,000
    (c) $125,000
    (d) $115,700

37. If an amount of $200 is received from Mr. Jones, but it is credited to Mr. James, what would this transaction affect?

    (a) Accounts of both James and Jones
    (b) Only cash accounts
    (c) Only the Jones accounts
    (d) Only the James accounts

38. Suppose a supplier gives a credit terms of "2/10, net 40". What would the approximate cost the buyer will bear by not taking the discount and paying at the end of credit period?

    (a) 18.6%
    (b) 24.3%
    (c) 24.8%
    (d) 30.0%

39. The future value of all cash inflow at the end of time horizon at a particular rate of interest calculated is a feature of:

    (a) Risk-free rate
    (b) Compounding method
    (c) Discounting
    (d) Risk Premium

40. Fixed-income security bonds that yield interest payments:

   (a) Irredeemable Bonds
   (b) Convertible Bonds
   (c) Redeemable Bonds
   (d) Deep Discount Bonds

41. James Housing negotiated a revolving credit agreement of $50,000 with Brans Bank. The agreement calls for an interest rate of 10% on fund use, 15% compensating balance and 1% commitment fee in the unused line of credit line. Assuming that compensating balance would not be maintained otherwise, what would be the effective annual interest cost if the company borrows $200,000 for one year:

   (a) 11.5%
   (b) 15%
   (c) 26.5%
   (d) 13.53%

Questions 42 – 44 are based on the scenario below:

Suppose that in 1995 the price index (base year 1992) was 110 and the income was $700 billion. The corresponding numbers for 1996 were 120 and $800 billion.

42. 1996 income expressed in 1992 dollars is:

   (a) less than $600B
   (b) $600B or more but not more than $700B
   (c) more than $700B but not more than $800B
   (d) more than $800B

43. 1996 income expressed in 1995 dollars is:

   (a) less than $600B
   (b) $600B or more but not more than $700B
   (c) more than $700B but not more than $800B
   (d) more than $800B

44. Inflation during 1996 was:

   (a) less than 10%
   (b) 10%
   (c) more than 10% but not more than 20%
   (d)

(e) more than 20%

45. Which is not a market entry strategy:

    (a) Licensing
    (b) Indirect exporting
    (c) Joint venture
    (d) International marketing

46. Information about physical working conditions, work scheduling including the organizational and social context of the job, is called:

    (a) Job context
    (b) Job specification
    (c) Work activities
    (d) HR policy manual

47. Management philosophy that requires employers to continuously set and relentlessly meet ever high quality, cost delivery and availability goals, is called:

    (a) Performance appraisal
    (b) Performance management
    (c) Continuous improvement
    (d) Management by objective

48. Beta is:

    (a) Measure of market risk
    (b) Measure of the systemic risk
    (c) Measure of total risk
    (d) All of above

49. A stock expected to pay a 1.00 dividend next year with a cost of capital 14% and zero growth rate would have a price of:

    (a) 7.14
    (b) 6.75
    (c) 11.9
    (d) 6.13

50. If the equity in total capital is 1/3, debt is 2/3 and return on equity is 15%, with debt of 10%, and corporate tax of 32%. What is the WACC?

(a) 10.53%
(b) 7.533%
(c) 9.533%
(d) 11.350%

51. A budget was estimated by a company for producing 500 C's and 300 D's for the coming next year. D's usually take twice the time to be made as it takes for C's.

Expected total fixed overheads are $102,000.

Cost relating to C's are as such:

Material	3000 Kg	$24000
Labor	2000 hours	$40000

Fixed overhead are to be absorbed on an hourly basis. Some of the material goes to waste which is estimated to be about 10% of the material purchased.

Absorption cost per unit of C is?

(a) $225.52
(b) $226.05
(c) $260.30
(d) $260.83

52. A company wants to improve its quality so it can raise it reputation and eventually raise its selling price. Current costs of the company are as follows:

	Old System	New System
Total Demand	3600 units	3600 units
Defects	20%	10%
Labor cost per unit	$35	$43
Material used per unit	3.2 Kg	3.5 Kg
Price/Kg of material	$3.2	$3.95
Overheads	$18000	$29560

Which of these options is nearest to the increase in selling price which can justify this?
    (a) $3.20
    (b) $9.80
    (c) $11.40
    (d) $15.00

53. The following are the results for the last year's production:

    Overhead budgeted = $8000
    Production budgeted = 4000 units
    Actual overheads = $8500
    Actual production = $3800

    What is under/over absorption?

    (a) $500 under absorption
    (b) $500 over absorption
    (c) $900 under absorption
    (d) $900 over absorption

54. In your duties as a manger providing financial statement analysis to your firm's executives you were asked to provide a vertical analysis. If the cost of goods was rounded to $240,000 and the firm's net sales were $480,000 what rounded percentage outcome of the vertical analysis would you present to your executives?

    (a) 40%
    (b) 24%
    (c) 50%
    (d) 20%

55. For the week ending June 30, Sara Workmann completed the following number of pieces: Monday 53; Tuesday 56; Wednesday 49; Thursday 54; and Friday 52. The piece rate is $.75. Find her total wages.

    (a) $216.15
    (b) $198.00
    (c) $198.75
    (d) $199.56

56. Your store sells a six-pack of soda pop for $2.70. This represents a saving of 10% off the individual price of a can of soda pop. Your regional manager wants you to sell individual cans without the 10% saving, so what would be the price a single can of soda pop?

    (a) $0.40
    (b) $0.35
    (c) $0.50
    (d) $0.55

57. Eight machines can produce 360 bottles per hour. If all the machines work at the same   rate, how many bottles could 5 such machines produce in 3 hours?

(a) 675
(b) 790
(c) 1,850
(d) 5,300

58. Amy's Family Lite Yogurt Company sells two popular favors, vanilla and almond. On Monday, the ratio of vanilla cones sold to almond cones sold was 2 to 3. If the business had sold 4 more vanilla cones, the ratio of vanilla cones sold to almond cones sold would have been 3 to 4. How many vanilla cones did the store sell on Monday?

(a) 33
(b) 32
(c) 42
(d) 43

59. Your discount carpet business normally sells all of its merchandise at a discount of 10% to 30% off the suggested retail price. If, during a special promotional sale, an additional 20% were to be deducted from the discounted price, what would be the lowest possible price of an item costing $260 before any discounts?

(a) $192.00
(b) $135.60
(c) $145.60
(d) $152.45

60. Your retail business receives a shipment of 1,000 dresses, for which you pay $9,000. You sell the dresses at a price 80% above the cost for one month, after which you reduce the price of the dresses to 20% above cost. Your store then sells 75% of the dresses during the first month and 50% of the remaining dresses afterward. How much gross income did sales of the dresses generate for you?

(a) $10,200
(b) $11,553
(c) $12,111
(d) $13,500

61. As a marketing manager your team has asked you to determine what percentage of Americans own both an automobile and a motorcycle. You determine that 75% of all Americans own an automobile and 15% own a motorcycle. But, 20% off all Americans own neither an automobile nor motorcycle. What is the percentage of Americans who own both?

(a) 2%
(b) 3%

(c) 5%
(d) 10%

62. A fashion company's spring season line for women utilizing a new soft fabric broke record sales last quarter. The company now plans to launch a line of clothing for men made with the same fabric. The company's plan assumes that:

(a) Women will plan to buy more clothing for themselves and their male partners
(b) Other companies will not make such a move
(c) Men will be as interested in the new soft fabric like the women were the year before
(d) The new line will replace declining markets

63. New technologies make it possible for customer service representatives to work from home, saving them extra time and money in commuting. They would likely increase productivity if the employees did not:

(a) Commute far
(b) Use cars verses other means of commuting
(c) Need to consult frequently with other colleagues to solve callers' issues
(d) Have pets at their home

64. One of your employees did not report that another worker stole company merchandise. The act of the employee who stole is unethical and perhaps a criminal violation if:

(a) The employee reported it
(b) The employee did not report it
(c) The employee reported it, or not
(d) The employee is caught and charged accordingly

65. Usually a successful year for a stock fund will result in an increased investor dollar flowing into the fund and increase in other mutual stocks offered by that same company. However, while last year JP Connor Mutual Company had one stock beat average market returns by a large margin, their other funds did not report an increase.

Which conclusion can best be drawn from the information above?

(a) When one stock fund beats the market the other is expected to follow
(b) The success of one fund is not the only factor affecting whether investors will invest in other funds by the same company
(c) The performance of JP Connor is unstable and investors should seek another company to invest with
(d) The market itself is unstable

66. Consumer research finds that the majority of televisions are purchased in the United States are by men. This appears to debunk the myth that women watch more television than men.

    This argument is flawed because:

    (a) It fails to differentiate between buying and using
    (b) It does not provide information about men and women in general
    (c) It is not statistical in nature
    (d) It is bias and likely not true

67. According to McCarthy, the "4Ps" of the *Marketing Mix* are generally known as:

    (a) Price, Platforms, Promotion, and Product
    (b) Price, Place, Promotion, and Product
    (c) Price, Place, Promotion, and Process
    (d) Price, Place, Program, and Product

68. As part of a marketing campaign to sell 10,000 1940 Ford truck replicas, what segments would best be targets for the most sales:

    (a) Gender, location, and eye color
    (b) Race, religion, location
    (c) Age, interest, and gender
    (d) Interest, race, job status

69. First buyers of new technologies are referred to in marketing as:

    (a) Geeks
    (b) First time buyers
    (c) Innovators
    (d) Test markets

70. The last buyers of technology are referred to in marketing as:

    (a) Slow movers
    (b) Laggards
    (c) Conservative shoppers
    (d) Isolated market

71. Focusing on what technologies the customer is currently using and how many of the products in the market the customer needs is what segmentation variable:

    (a) Demographic variable
    (b) Personal variable
    (c) Situational variable

(d) Operating variable

72. The use of secondary data is preferred over primary data because it is:

(a) More cost effective and quick
(b) More scientific
(c) More reliable
(d) More understandable

73. What type of organization would most be preferred if you wanted a structure that facilitated the horizontal flow of skills and information and your main idea was in the management of large projects or product development processes, drawing employees from different functional disciplines for assignment to a team without removing them from their respective positions:

(a) Simple
(b) Functional (U-Form)
(c) Multidivisional (M-form)
(d) Matrix

74. Newskin, Inc. is marketing a new face cream that is very expensive but expects wide sales anyway because of the notion it will make buyers look years younger. This pricing is based on what type of tactic:

(a) Value pricing
(b) Flat rate pricing
(c) Direct price discrimination
(d) Complementary pricing

75. Jell-O brand gelatin offering Jell-O Pudding Ice-pops is an example of what marketing strategy:

(a) Branding
(b) Brand extension
(c) Brand expansion
(d) Brand reconditioning

76. Setting up tables or booths in a grocery store and allowing customers to try products for free is what type of marketing promotion strategy:

(a) Premium strategy
(b) Sampling strategy
(c) Direct marketing strategy
(d) Product promotion strategy

77. What statement is most true of teams:

    (a) Teams are made up of people who agree on how things should get done
    (b) Teams are highly interdependent and cannot function when the members have multiple subtasks.
    (c) Teams are comprised of groups of people linked to a common purpose and conduct tasks that are high in complexity and have many interdependent subtasks
    (d) Teams need to function with uncommon tasks because that's why they are a team because its diversity that bonds them together

78. What is the most likely outcome of internal recruitment for upper mobility positions:

    (a) Will act to deter those who are not hired to apply again
    (b) Will upset the majority of staff in the organization
    (c) Will draw scandals from outside employment agencies
    (d) Will act as an incentive for staff to work harder within the organization

79. What is the most likely reason to recruit externally:

    (a) To find new talent and to bring new ideas and energy to the organization
    (b) To upset internal staff so they make changes
    (c) To create employee competition
    (d) To meet requests and receive incentives of outside recruiters and headhunters

80. The most important outcome in favor of the organization for increasing an employee's compensation regularly is:

    (a) The employee's internal sense of accomplishment
    (b) The employee's increase in productivity
    (c) The employee's personal satisfaction
    (d) The employee's thankfulness to management

81. The "product concept" is most likely synonymous to:

    (a) Price
    (b) Quality
    (c) Market Value
    (d) Idea

82. The "selling concept" is most likely synonymous to:

    (a) Hard sales
    (b) A product selling itself
    (c) Sales being inevitable

(d) Sales based on a bargain

83. Due to a legal regulation, Don's Digital Signs was unable to advertise and market in a way they wished. What type of variable, beyond Don's control, created this issue?

(a) Marketing variable
(b) Exogenous variable
(c) External variable
(d) Regulatory variable

84. Mr. Rollen wants to market a new product that appears more advantageous to potential customers than competing brands. The rate of adoption of a new offering therefore depends on the product's:

(a) Cost savings
(b) Relative advantage
(c) Market share
(d) Warranty

85. Marketing in a way to get customers to buy a product despite the fact that it may not necessarily be good for them (e.g. foods high in fat content) is the ability to help them work through this condition:

(a) Guilt
(b) Social pressure
(c) Cognitive dissonance
(d) Manipulation

86. Scott wants to do market research on religious beliefs and opinions of clergy. What dimension of segmentation is Scott looking at:

(a) Demographic
(b) Usage
(c) Sector
(d) Psychographic

87. While doing an analysis of the product life cycle for Product "A" you notice that several other companies have market share for the same product and that Product "A" has been suffering declines in sales. What would be a reasonable recommendation to make

(a) File for bankruptcy
(b) Abandonment. Go out of business to avoid further decline
(c) Cut costs and offer a new product

(d) Merge with another company

88. Your company made a purchase of $80,000 in equipment that has a life span of 4 years. Using a straight-line method of measuring depreciation, what is the amount you can depreciate for each of the 4 years?

(a) $10,000
(b) $15,000
(c) $20,000
(d) $32,000

89. An investment of $200,000 is expected to generate the following cash flows in six years:

Year	Net cash flow
1	$30,000
2	$40,000
3	$60,000
4	$70,000
5	$55,000
6	$45,000

What would be the payback period of the investment?

(a) 3 years
(b) 4 years
(c) 5 years
(d) 6 years

90. If your company's current assets are $40 million and current liabilities are $48 million what is the current ratio?

(a) 0.83
(b) 0.88
(c) 0.90
(d) 1.00

91. Based on the current ratio found in question #90 above, what should the company do?

(a) Borrow
(b) Restructure debt
(c) Sell stock
(d) Keep doing what they are doing

92. Your company's net income is $8.5 million and the shareholder's equity is $145 million therefore the return on equity is:

   (a) 17.5%
   (b) 59%
   (c) 5%
   (d) 5.9%

93. According to *Standard and Poor's* (S&P) the highest rating a bond can achieve is:

   (a) A+
   (b) AA
   (c) AAA
   (d) AAAA

94. A manager who rewards and gives important titles to employees will likely satisfy what Maslow's hierarchy of need:

   (a) Level 1: Survival
   (b) Level 2: Safety
   (c) Level 3: Belonging
   (d) Level 4: Self-Esteem

95. Ms. Rose feels that if she is benevolent to her employees they will like her and do what she tells to do is likely to use what type of management style:

   (a) Autocratic
   (b) Custodial
   (c) Participative
   (d) Collegial

96. The cost savings that result from dealing in larger quantities, can be increased to the extent that fixed costs (those not sensitive to variations in volume) are absorbed by each additional unit that is produced or purchased is known in operational management as:

   (a) Economies of scale
   (b) Economies of supply
   (c) Economies of volume
   (d) Economies of quantity

97. Mr. Jones wants to determine at what point the company should switch from one product to a competing other. What tool should he use?

   (a) Cost analysis
   (b) Cluster analysis

    (c) Crossover analysis
    (d) Point analysis

98. What type of research data collection method would likely yield the least amount of responses?

    (a) Focus groups
    (b) Mailing
    (c) Telephoning
    (d) In person

99. Which method would likely yield the greater opportunity for interviewer cheating?

    (a) Focus groups
    (b) Mailing
    (c) Telephoning
    (d) In person

100. The 2009 balance sheet of Carlo's Marina Shop showed long-term debt of $3.2 million, and the 2010 balance sheet showed long-term debt of $3.9 million. The 2010 income statement showed an interest expense of $750,000.

The firm's cash flow to creditors during 2010 is _____?

    (a) $50,000
    (b) $55,000
    (c) $45,000
    (d) $51,500

101. The market value balance sheet for Jules Manufacturing is shown here:

Market Value Balance Sheet			
Cash	$219,000	Debt	$184,000
Fixed assets	380,000	Equity	415,000
Total	$599,000	Total	$599,000

Jules has declared a 22% stock dividend. The stock goes ex dividend tomorrow (the chronology for a stock dividend is similar to that for a cash dividend).

If there are 17,000 shares outstanding, the stock price today is _____?

(a) $23.4
(b) $24.4
(c) $25.5
(d) $25.4

102. You own 1,000 shares of stock in Beal's Corporation. You will receive a $0.75 per share dividend in one year. In two years, Beal's will pay a liquidating dividend of $40 per share. The required return on Beal's stock is 16 percent. Suppose you want only $190 total in dividends the first year, show how you can accomplish this by creating homemade dividends. Your total dividend amount in year 2 will be _____?

(a) $40,655.7
(b) $40,649.6
(c) $41,678.7
(d) $42,675.9

103. You own a portfolio that has $1,400 invested in Stock A and $1,900 invested in Stock B. If the expected returns on these stocks are 11 percent and 13 percent, respectively, the expected return on the portfolio is _____percent?

(a) 11.15
(b) 13.33
(c) 14.90
(d) 12.15

104. Human resource managers are often asked to provide information in various ways to the organization. If the total work carried out by part-time workers is equal to 120 hours per week, and a full-time worker's is 30, then the full-time equivalent (FTE) of all part-time workers would be?

(a) 2
(b) 3
(c) 4
(d) 5

Questions 105 – 109 are based on the following:

The EPA estimated that replacing the 24,000 feet of pipe will cut cost at the community X water pumping operations. It would cost $5.00 per foot of pipe to fix. After the replacement, yearly cost savings will equal 52% of old cost. This will reduce the overall water loss therefore, reducing the volume of water withdrawn, treated, and pumped from the reservoir per year. Additional benefits include reductions in unnecessary pumping and operation and maintenance expenditures, and eliminating potential health hazards associated with waterborne pathogens entering the water distribution system. The original annual costs were $200,100 a year.

105. What would the new cost per year be?

    (a) $175, 950
    (b) $96,098
    (c) $104,052
    (d) $200,100

106. What would be the cost to fix the entire pipe?

    (a) $200,000
    (b) $120,000
    (c) $100,000
    (d) $600,000

107. Not including the cost to fix the pipe, what would be the actual cost savings for water pumping operations yearly?

    (a) $156,000
    (b) $150,000
    (c) $116,338
    (d) $104,052

108. How much would the utility lose if they did not fix the pipe for the next 5 years considering prices did not increase?

    (a) $279,750
    (b) $113,550
    (c) $400,260
    (d) $230,240

109. Considering the long-term view of five years and short-term view of one year, should they replace the pipe?

    (a) No, for long-term; Yes, for short term
    (b) No, for short-term; Yes, for long-term
    (c) No, for both
    (d) Yes, for both

Questions 110 – 113 are based on the following:

Asda is a UK retailer focused on selling food, clothing, electronics, toys, home furnishings and general merchandise. Asda also offers a range of additional services such as 'Asda Money' financial services. In 1999 Asda became a subsidiary of Walmart, the largest supermarket chain in the world. This enabled Walmart to enter the UK market but also gave Asda access to the full range of expertise of the Walmart company. Walmart currently employs over 2 million colleagues worldwide in 27 countries. In the UK, Asda is one of the largest employers with over 175,000 colleagues working across its many formats. These include a variety of roles in its Superstores, Supermarkets, Home Office, Distribution, George and Asda Living. Asda continues to expand its operations in the UK and recently acquired a number of stores from Netto to increase the number of local Asda Supermarkets. Asda also funds research to find out why things go wrong in pregnancy and birth, and provides information free of charge

110. Asda's funding of research to find out why things go wrong in pregnancy and birth, and providing information free of charge is an example of:

(a) Ethical mandate
(b) Corporate social responsibility
(c) Company investment
(d) Public and relations

111. Why is Asda and Walmart most likely a success:

(a) Advertising methods
(b) Store locations
(c) USA – UK connection
(d) Supply chain -- Wal-Mart has the power to squeeze profit-killing concessions from vendors.

112. In what key way does Asda keep its competitive advantage?

(a) By providing the most goods at the least cost
(b) By Providing a strong work force (Asda is the largest employers of Walmart with over 175,000 colleagues working across its many formats).
(c) By offering a range of services (e.g. financial services) and keeping a variety of roles in its Superstores, Supermarkets, Home Office, Distribution, George and Asda Living and expanding its operations in the UK and recently acquired a number of stores from Netto.
(d) By offering information free of charge.

113. Walmart acquiring Asda was likely conducted with their motive to produce what end result?

(a) To increase higher competition in international retail
(b) To increased American business models in UK
(c) Offer low cost goods at a discount to other countries
(d) Increase overall market share

Questions 114 – 116 are based on the following:

Kellogg created All-Bran as a product and the fiber sector of the cereal market in the 1930s. From then onwards the product experienced steady growth with the company injecting regular promotional spends to support product development. The most spectacular growth was in the 1980s with widespread publicity for the 'F' Plan Diet from nutritionists and health experts. This diet had an impact similar to that of the Atkins Diet in recent years. Following this, the Kellogg 'bran' range has been moving into a more mature stage. Kellogg's market research showed that, in choosing a cereal product, consumers place high priority on taste. Although they want a healthier cereal, it still must taste good.

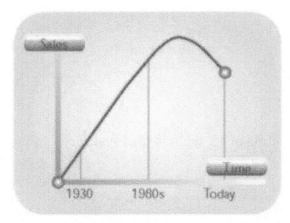

Read more: http://businesscasestudies.co.uk/kelloggs/building-a-brand-in-order-to-sustain-its-life-cycle/all-brans-product-life-cycle.html#ixzz3ANPH6bRx

114. What should Kellogg do to avoid moving to a decline and possible extinction?

(a) Change the parent brand name to create new interests
(b) Re-brand a range of fiber cereals developing new 'tastier' products under the single All-Bran umbrella to renewed growth and interest.
(c) Merge with other cereal companies
(d) Market to the segment who is older and more willing to purchase the product

115. To give a selling campaign the maximum impact, Kellogg should?

(a) Carefully coordinated television and radio advertising, PR and in-store promotions. These encouraged consumers to try out and reappraise the revamped products.
(b) Go door-to-door to show people that Kellogg is personal and friendly.
(c) Calling segments to notify them of changes. This shows customers that Kellogg cares enough to call them. This will get them to buy.
(d) Advertising in local papers because most people look there to get information about what's new.

116. If Kellogg wants to make their product's total sales grow, they must?

(a) Sell at the lowest cost
(b) Get the most customers
(c) Provide the best quality at the lowest cost
(d) Carefully consider how best to extend its life cycle

117. Calculate the operating income for Alpha company based on the following:

Revenue $1M
Costs $500,000
Labor $300,000
Admin exp. $100,000

(a) $100,000
(b) $200,000
(c) $400,000
(d) 500,000

118. If 502 bits were tested accurate out of a sample of 48, what is the inventory accuracy?

(a) 502
(b) 454
(c) 48
(d) 10

119. Consider that 317 total number of direct hours were invested. What is the output per direct labor hour if 465 units were completed, along with 310 total unit equivalents and 110 total carryforward unit equivalents?

(a) 1.79
(b) 2.00
(c) 2.09
(d) 4.65

120. According to Lewin's theory of change, what stage occurs when changes are accepted and therefore become the new norm?

(a) Change
(b) Unfreeze
(c) Freeze
(d) Frozen

121. Mr. Lowe's new job involves oversight of materials, information, and finances as they move in a process from supplier to manufacturer to wholesaler to retailer to consumer. His main task is to reduce inventory. It is best if he has experience in what type of management?

(a) Change management
(b) Risk management
(c) Senior management
(d) Supply chain management

Answer Key

Answer Key

1. b
2. c
3. a
4. d
5. c
6. a
7. b
8. c
9. b
10. b
11. a
12. c
13. d
14. d
15. d
16. a
17. c
18. d*
19. a
20. b*
21. a*
22. d
23. c
24. a
25. d
26. b*
27. b*
28. d
29. b
30. b*
31. a*
32. a
33. a*
34. a*
35. d
36. a*
37. a
38. c*
39. c
40. b
41. d*
42. b*
43. c*

44. a*
45. d
46. b
47. c
48. b
49. a*
50. c*
51. b*
52. b
53. c*
54. c*
55. b*
56. c*
57. a*
58. b*
59. c*
60. d*
61. d*
62. c
63. c
64. c
65. b
66. a
67. b
68. c
69. c
70. b
71. d
72. a
73. d
74. a
75. b
76. b
77. c
78. d
79. a
80. b
81. b
82. a
83. b
84. b
85. c
86. d
87. c
88. c*
89. b

90. a*
91. b
92. d*
93. c
94. d
95. b
96. a
97. c
98. b
99. d
100. a*
101. b*
102. b*
103. d*
104. c*
105. b*
106. b*
107. d*
108. c*
109. b*
110. b
111. d
112. c
113. d
114. b
115. a
116. d
117. a*
118. b*
119. c*
120. c
121. d

*See corresponding solution below:

* <u>Solutions for Mathematical Questions</u>

Question 18. Answer: (d)

Initial Cost: $3800
Income each year: $1000
No. of Years: 5

NPV = PV of all positive cashflows – Initial Investment

PV of First year inflow = $1000*0.926= $926
PV of Second Year Inflow = $1000*0.857 = $857
PV of Third Year Inflow = $1000*0.794 = $794
PV of Fourth Year Inflow = $1000*0.735 = $735
PV of Fifth Year Inflow = $1000*0.681= $681

So NPV = ($926+$857+$794+$735+$681)-$3800 = $193

Yes, since NPV is greater than 0 the project should be accepted.

Question 20. Answer: (b)

Invested capital = $96,000,000
Return on investment = 18%
So, target annual income = $96,000,000*0.18 = $17,280,000

Question 21. Answer: (a)

Total Fixed Cost = $170,000+$48,000+$122,000 = $340000

Question 26. Answer: (b)

Tax Saving on the loss = Loss Amount * Tax Rate
Tax Saving on the loss = $33500*40% = $13400

Question 27. Answer: (b)

ROI = Income/Investment
ROI = 6,000,000 Pesos/30,000,000 = 20%

Question 30. Answer: (b)

Right can be exercised on 5th share

Theoretical value of right = (Stock Price - Rights subscription price per share) / (Number of rights required to buy one share + 1)

Theoretical value of right = ($60-$54)/(4+1) = $1.20

Question 31. Answer (a)

Theoretical value of Right (calculated in previous problem) = $1.2
Share Price before right = $60
Share price after it goes ex right =$60 - $1.2 = $58.8

Another Method

Share price after it goes ex right = (share price before right * number of shares + right subscription share price * no of share) / total number of shares
Share price after it goes ex right = (60*4+54*1)/5 = (294/5) = $58.8

Question 33. Answer: (a)

If discount is taken then payment would be made in 10 days. As purchase was made on 21st Oct then payment would be made on 1st Nov.

If discount is not taken then payment would be made after 30 days. As purchase was made on 20st Nov then payment would be made on 1st Nov.

Question 34. Answer: (a)

GDP Deflator = (Nominal GDP/Real GDP)*100

As we are calculating GDP Deflator for used in revision so we will take revised values.

GDP Deflator = ($4.523/$3.877)*100

GDP Deflator = 116.66

Question 36. Answer: (a)

Liabilities = Assets – Owner's Equity

Liabilities = $99,500 - $50,500

Liabilities = $ 49000

Question 38. Answer: (c)

Cost to the Buyer = Discount %/(100 – Discount %)x (365/(Full allowed payment days –Discount days))

Cost to the Buyer = 2%/(100%-2%)x (365/(40-10))

Cost to the Buyer = 2%/98% x (365/30)

Cost to the buyer = 0.0204 * (365/30) = 24.83%

Question 41. Answer: (d)

Effective Annual Interest Cost = (Interest Cost + Commitment fee)/(amount borrowed – compensating balance)

Interest cost = $200,000 * 0.1 = $20,000

Commitment fee = ($500,000 - $200,000)*0.01 = $3000

Compensating balance = borrowed amount * compensating rate

Compensating balance = $200,000 * 0.15 = $30,000

So, Effective annual interest cost = ($20,000 + 3,000)/($200,000 - $30,000) =

13.53%

Question 42. Answer: (b)

Current year = 1996

Base year = 1992

Current price index = 120

So, Current price index/base price index = current income/current year income expressed in base year

120/100 = 800/current income expressed in base year

So, 1996 income expressed in base year numbers would be = 100/120*$800 = $666.67

So, more than $600, but less than $700.

Question 43. Answer: (c)

So, current price index/1995 price index = current income/current income expressed in 1995.

120/110 = 800/current income expressed in 1995

Current income expressed in 1995 = $800 * 110/120 =$733

So, it is greater than $700, but less than $800

Question 44. Answer: (a)

Current year inflation = (current price index/last year price index) – 1

Inflation = (120/110)-1

Inflation = 1.0909 -1 = 0.0909 =9.09 %

So, it is less than 10%

Question 49. Answer: (a)

Share Price = Next year dividend / (cost of capital – growth rate)

Share Price = 1.00/(0.14-0)

Share Price = 7.14

Question 50. Answer: (c)

WACC = (equity weight*cost of equity)+(debt weight*cost of debt*(1-tax rate))

WACC = (1/3*15%)+(2/3*10%*(1-32%))

WACC = 5% + 4.53%

WACC = 9.533%

Question 51. Answer is (b)

Material Cost Per Kg = $24000/3000= $8

Material Needed for C = 3000 Kg, Expected wastage 10% of the purchase.
So material need to be purchased for C = 3000/(1-10%)=3333.33
Total Material Cost = 3333.3333*$8= $26667

Material cost per unit = $26667/500 = $53.33
Labor Cost Per Unit = $40000/500 = $80
Total Fixed head cost = $102,000

Total Hours per Unit product for C = 2000/500= 4 Hour
Total Hours per Unit product for D = 4*2 = 8 Hour
Total Hours worked for C = 4*500= 2000 Hours
Total Hours worked for D = 8*300= 2400 Hours
Fixed cost per hour = $102,000/(2000+2400)= $23.18

Fixed cost for C = $23.18*2000= $46363
Fixed cost per Unit = $46363/500= $92.73
Absorption Cost per Unit = Material cost per unit + Labor cost per unit + Fixed Cost per Unit

Absorption Cost Per Unit = $53.33+$80+$92.73 = $226.05

Question 52. Answer: (b)

Total Cost per Unit for Old System

Total Demand = 3600 Units, Defects = 20%

So units need to be produced: 3600/(1-20%) = 4500

Total Labor cost = $35*4500= $157,500

Material cost per unit = $3.2*3.2 = $10.24

Total Material Cost = $10.24*4500= $46080

Overhead = $18000

Total Cost = $157500+$46080+$18000= $221,580
Cost per Unit= $221,580/3600= $61.55

Total Cost per Unit for New System

Total Demand = 3600 Units, Defects = 10%
So units need to be produced: 3600/(1-10%) = 4000
Total Labor cost = $43*4000= $172,000

Material cost per unit = $3.95*3.5 = $13.825
Total Material Cost = $13.825*4000= $55,300
Overhead = $29,560

Total Cost = $172,000+$55,300+$29,560= $256,860
Cost per Unit= $256,860/3600= $71.35

Increase in cost which would justify increase in Price =$71.35-$61.55 = $9.80

Question 53. Answer: (c)

Budgeted Per Unit overhead = $8000/4000 = $2

Actual Production = 3800 units

Budgeted overhead on Actual Production = 3800*$2 = $7600

Actual overhead = $8500

As budget is lower than actual so it would be under absorption.

Under absorption = $8500 -$7600 = $900

Question 54. Answer: (c)

COGS Vertical Analysis = Cost of Goods Sold/Net Sales

COGS Vertical Analysis = $240,000/$480,000 = 50%

Question 55. Answer: (b)

Total Wages = Total hours worked * rate

Total Hours worked = 53+56+49+54+52 = 264

Rate = $0.75

Total Wages = 264*$.75 = $198

Question 56. Answer: (c)

Price of six cans = $2.70

Price of single can = $2.7/6 = $0.45

Saving = 10%

So, price without saving = price with saving/(1-saving rate)

Price without saving = $0.45/(1-0.1) = $0.5

Question 57. Answer: (a)

Eight machines produce 360 bottles per hour

So, one machine produces 360/8 = 45 bottles per hour

Five machines produce 45*5= 225 bottles per hour

So, five machines production in three hours = 225*3=675

Question 58. Answer: (b)

Assume store sold 2x vanilla cones on Monday,
So, almond cones sold were 3x

If store had sold 4 more vanilla cones then sold vanilla cones would be 2x+4 and ratio would have been 3 to 4.

So, using the equation

$(2x+4)/3x = ¾$

Using the crossing method

$4*(2x+4) = 3*3x$
$8x+16=9x$ so $x = 16$

Number of vanilla cones sold on Monday = 16*2 = 32

Question 59. Answer: (c)

Lowest possible price = Highest discount

Highest discount rate = 30%

So, Price before any discount = $260

First highest discount = 30%

Price after first discount = $260*(1-30%) = $182

Additional discount rate = 20%

Price after additional discount = $182*(1-20%)

Price after additional discount = $145.60

Question 60. Answer: (d)

Cost of 1000 dresses = $9000
Per dress cost = $9000/1000 = $9

Price in first month (80% above cost) = $9*(1+80%) = $16.2
Price after first month (20% above cost) = $9*(1+20%) = $10.8

Sales during first month (75% of total dresses) = 1000*75% = 750
Sales after first month (50% of remaining dresses) = (1000-750)*50%= 125

Income = Sales * Price
Income in first month = 750*$16.2 = $12150
Income after first month = 125* $10.8 = $1350

Total Income = $12150 +$1350 = $13500

Question 61. Answer: (d)

Percentage of Americans who own neither = 20%
So, Percentage of Americans who at least own one = 1-20% = 80%

Percentage of Americans who own a motorcycle = 15%

Percentage of American who own an automobile = 75%

So, Percentage of Americans who own both = Percentage of American who own a motorcycle + Percentage of American who own an automobile - Percentage of Americans who at least own one

Percentage of Americans who own both = 15% + 75% - 80% = 10%

Question 88. Answer: (c)

Straight line depreciation = (Purchase price – salvage value)/No of years
Straight line depreciation = ($80000-0)/4 =$20000

Question 89. Answer: (b)

Year	Net cash flow	Cumulative Cash flow
1	$30,000	$30,000
2	$40,000	$70,000
3	$60,000	$130,000
4	$70,000	$200,000
5	$55,000	$255,000
6	$45,000	$300,000

Payback period = Year at which cumulative Cash flow and Initial investment are same.

So, Payback Period = 4 Years

Question 90. Answer: (a)

Current Ratio = Current assets/ Current liabilities

Current Ratio = $40/$48 = 0.83

Question 92. Answer: (d)

Return on Equity = Net income/Shareholder's equity

Return on Equity = $8.5/$145 = 5.9%

Question 100: Answer (a)

Cash flow to creditors = Decrease in long term loan + interest payment

Cash flow to creditors = ($3.2-$3.9) +$0.75

Cash flow to creditors = -$0.7 + $0.75 = $0.05 million = $50,000

Question 101. Answer: (b)

As stock goes ex dividend tomorrow so today's price won't have any effect of stock dividend.

So, Stock price = Equity/No of Shares

Stock Price = $415,000/17,000 = $24.41

Question 102. Answer: (b)

Price of Share today = expected present value of all future cash flow

Expected cash flow in one year = $0.75 per share
PV of expected cash flow in one year = $0.75/1.16 = $0.647

Expected cash flow in second year = $40 per share
PV of expected cash flow in second year = $40/(1.16)^2 = $29.726

Price of stock today = $0.647+$29.726 = $30.373

So, if I only $190 dividend in first year, that would make $190/1000 = $0.19 dividend/Share

Using the same price today,
Price of stock today = PV of expected cash flow in first year + PV of expected cash flow in second year

$30.373 = ($0.19/1.16) + (D/1.16^2)
$30.373 = $0.1637 + (D/1.3456)
D= ($30.373-$0.1637)*1.3456 = $40.649
So, dividend on 1000 Shares would be $40.649*1000 = $40,649

Question 103. Answer: (d)

Weight of stock A = 1400/(1400+1900) = 0.424 = 42.4%

Weight of Stock B = 1 - 42.4%= 0.576 =57.6%

Expected return on portfolio = (Weight of stock A*return on stock A) + (weight of stock B*return on stock B)

Expected return on portfolio = (42.4% * 11%) + (57.6%+13%)

Expected return on portfolio = 4.664% + 7.488% = 12.152%

Question 104. Answer: (c)

Full-time worker hours = 30

Part-time workers' total hours = 120

So, Full-time equivalent of all part-time workers = 120/30 = 4

So, 4 full-time workers can cover the work of all part-time workers.

Question 105. Answer: (b)

Total cost before fixing pipe = $200,100

Saving = 52% of total cost

Saving = $200,100*0.52 = $104,052

So new cost = old cost – Saving

New Cost = $201,100 - $104,052

New Cost = $96,098 per year

Question 106. Answer: (b)

Total pipe feet = 24,000

Cost per foot = $5

Total cost = total feet of pipe * cost per foot

Total cost = 24000*$5 = $120,000

Question 107. Answer: (d)

Cost Saving = Old cost – new cost

Cost Saving = $200,100 - $96,048 = 104,052

OR

Cost Saving = old cost * cost saving percentage

Cost Saving = $200,100*0.52 = $104,052

Question108. Answer: (c)

Total loss for five years = total saving for five years – cost to fix the pipe

Total saving for five years = saving per year * no of years

Total saving for five years = $104,052 * 5 = $520,260

Total loss for five years = $520,260 - $120,000 = $400,260

Question 109. Answer: (b)

Pipe fixing cost is a one-time cost and Annual cost is a recurring cost. So, if it is for one year then total gain/ (loss) would be = $104,052 - $120,000 = -15,948

If it is for five years then total gain/ (loss) would be = $520,260 - $120,000= $400,260

As one-year profit is negative and five years profit is in positive, they should only change the pipe if it is long term project.

Question 117. Answer: (a)

Operating income = Operating Revenue – Total Operating cost

Total Operating cost = $500,000+$300,000+$100,000 = $900,000

Operating Income = $1,000,000 - $900,000 = $100,000

Question 118. Answer: (b)

Bit record = 502

Real quantity = 48

Mean Absolute Error = | Qe - Qr |

Mean Absolute Error = |502-48|

Inventory accuracy using MAE = 454

Question 119. Answer: (c)

Total Hours Invested = 317

Units Completed = 465

Other units equivalents = 310

Carry forward units = 110

Total Units = Units completed + other units equivalents – carry forward units

Total Units = 465+310-110 = 665

Output per unit = Total Units/total hours

Out per unit = 665/317 = 2.09

References and suggested readings

Bloomsbury Information Ltd. (2010). *Pocket dictionary of business.* London, England: Author.

Datar, S. M., & Rajan, M. V. (2014). *Managerial accounting.* Upper Saddle River, NJ: Pearson.

ETS® Major Field Test for the MBA website (n.d.). ETS® Major Field Test for the MBA. Retrieved from, https://www.ets.org/mft/about/content/mba

ETS® Major Field Test for the MBA website (n.d.). ETS® Major Field Test in Master of Business Administration Sample Questions. Retrieved from, https://www.ets.org/Media/Tests/MFT/pdf/mft_samp_questions_mba.pdf

Griffin, M. (2009). *MBA fundamentals: Accounting and finance.* New York, NY: Kaplan Publishing.

Ross, S., Westerfield, R., Jaffe, J., & Bradford, J. (2010). *Corporate finance: Core principles and applications* (3rd ed). New York: McGraw-Hill Irwin.

Salzman, S. A., Miller, C. D. & Clendenen, G. (2001). *Mathematics business.* Boston, MA: Addison-Wesley Longman.

Schoenebeck, K. P., & Holtzman, M. P. (2013). *Interpreting and analyzing financial statements: A project-based approach* (6th ed). Upper Saddle River, NJ: Pearson.

Sutherland, J, & Canwell, D. (2004). *Key concepts in accounting and finance.* New York, NY: Palgrave Macmillan

Sutherland, J, & Canwell, D. (2004). *Key concepts in business practice.* New York, NY: Palgrave Macmillan.

Notes

Notes

Notes

Notes

Notes

Notes

Notes

Made in the
USA
Middletown, DE

76701320R00091